So You Want to Be a Teacher?

D0321026

Also available from Continuum

*How to Survive Your First Year in Teaching
(2nd edition)* – Sue Cowley

100 Ideas for Trainee Teachers – Angella Cooze

Primary Teacher's Handbook (2nd edition) – Lyn Overall and
Margaret Sangster

Secondary Teacher's Handbook (2nd edition) – Lyn Overall and
Margaret Sangster

How to be a Successful Secondary Teacher – Sue Leach

Inside Guide to Training as a Teacher – Jon Barbuti

Getting the Buggers to Behave (3rd edition) – Sue Cowley

Trainee Teacher's Survival Guide (2nd edition) – Hazel Bennett

*Everything You Need to Know to Survive Teaching
(2nd edition)* – The Ranting Teacher

Available from Network Continuum

Pocket PAL: Newly Qualified Teachers – Henry Liebling

So You Want to Be a Teacher?

a Teacher?

How to Launch Your Teaching Career

LUCY WAIDE

continuum

ABERDEENSHIRE LIBRARY INFORMATION SERVICES	
2649358	
HJ	2287356
371.425	£12.99
	ANF

Continuum International Publishing Group

The Tower Building
11 York Road
London SE1 7NX

80 Maiden Lane
Suite 704
New York, NY 10038

www.continuumbooks.com

© Lucy Waide 2008

All rights reserved. No part of this publication may be reproduced or transmitted in any form or by any means, electronic or mechanical, including photocopying, recording, or any information storage or retrieval system, without prior permission in writing from the publishers.

Lucy Waide has asserted her right under the Copyright, Designs and Patents Act, 1988, to be identified as Author of this work.

British Library Cataloguing-in-Publication Data
A catalogue record for this book is available from the British Library.

ISBN: 978-1-84706-023-5 (paperback)

Library of Congress Cataloging-in-Publication Data
Waide, Lucy.

So you want to be a teacher? : how to launch your teaching career/ Lucy Waide.

p. cm. – (So you want to be?)
ISBN 978-1-84706-023-5 (pbk.)
1. Teaching – Vocational guidance – Great Britain. I. Title. II. Series.

LB1775.4.G7W35 2008
371.1002'3 – dc22   2008034708

Typeset by Newgen Imaging Systems Pvt Ltd, Chennai, India
Printed and bound in Great Britain by Ashford Press

So you want to be . . .

Advice to be taken with as many grains of salt as you wish.

Be warned, there will be many analogies to driving a car, and many anecdotes referring to English!

Contents

on the people who are important. Making any impression in a large school is difficult, if you are to be remembered, you need to know how to make yourself indispensable.

This is your homework that lasts for a year. It is always put on a pedestal by tutors, and as with all students, the thought that bare minimum will suffice is always at the forefront. Helpful tips allow both the conscientious and the bone idle to find a pathway. Organizing yourself and making sure you are able to keep on top of the workload through making lists.

Understanding that you have to meet certain standards. Realizing that some are obvious to your development as a teacher, and some are just to jump through a hoop. What happens upon reaching the ultimate goal? This chapter provides a few little hints as to how to milk this precious year for all it's worth and what it actually means for your progression. Moving Up the Ladder.

The pitfalls of climbing up too fast, or too slowly. A few tips on how to have a steady climb.

How to cope with the drone of information being read out and how to show willing when the will to live is leaving. Finding a voice and how to ensure you're confident with it rather than arrogant and argumentative.

Housekeeping: Get your house in order! Keeping yourself organized will help you to keep yourself sane. Make sure you don't go into a huge panic when you are asked for that little piece of paper you were handed three weeks ago in passing.

Starter – Preface

When you first decide to embark on the rollercoaster of education it is imperative that you do your own homework before giving it out yourself. You will be expected to wear many hats and to pretty much have a controlled version of schizophrenia. However, all this being said, teaching can be an incredibly gratifying and rewarding profession. Take heed though, the term 'caring profession' may not always refer to the caring of **other** people.

I was in training myself for four years! This wasn't due to any inadequacy on my behalf before you think 'bloody hell how crap is she?' I began my marathon training session in September of 2001 to become a teacher in the post-16 sector. I then moved on in September 2002 to a secondary school after receiving a phone call inviting me to work there. This isn't the regular way of getting a job in a school; I always say teaching chose me rather than the other way round. I didn't embark on a proper training programme until January 2003 as a GTP student. On successful completion of this and after numerous moments of insanity, I embarked on my NQT year in January 2004, in which I became a coach for GTP students, and later with NQTs. I therefore had three September starts as a trainee, and feel quite able to pass on a little of what I learned during that time about being a 'Teacher in Training', and a little of the learning thereafter.

I now teach in a special school as Head of the Art Department and feel that no matter where you teach or who you teach, as long as you take part in some of the learning as you go along and make sure you realize that you will never stop learning you should develop skills throughout your career.

I have found teaching to be both a rewarding and depressing profession at times, as we will all experience in our lives, whatever jobs we choose to dabble in. It does get easier, but on the other hand the rose-tinted glasses gradually fade every year you're in it. As long as you can take the rough with the smooth and get out a little smile about something each day, you'll get by quite nicely.

1 | Why would you want to teach?

WE NEED YOU (AND YOUR BISCUITS)

Some people are drawn to it. Some people are chosen to do it. Some people were predestined to do it. Some were just after the good wage and holiday package. Me? I was lured into teaching at a point in my life at which I was at a crossroads. Data input by night and cleaner/receptionist/nanny/student by day meant I was so busy, I thought (naively) that I would welcome the time to just explore, analyse, lose and find myself. Within two weeks I was so mind-numbingly bored with my new freedom I actually longed for some structure and regulation to my days. I didn't particularly know what I wanted to do. Teaching in a secondary school had never entered my mind. Obviously I was leaning towards working within the education sector as I had just completed a year of Post-16 Teacher Training in Art; however I had never EVER even had the slightest want, inclination, desire, or ambition to teach English in a secondary school. It was pure fluke that I happened to check my old mobile phone (that I was in the middle of transferring) for answer machine messages, on which was an invitation to come and work at the school on the GTP Programme.

The main reason for my introduction to the terrifying teaching world was simply, 'Why not?' Looking back now it must have been something more. I treated going into teaching with the same amount of trepidation as I would when deciding between one piece of chocolate and the bar. Obviously, in this instance the 'Why not?' is answered with: because you'll turn into a big fat heifer and you will be ruining all of the hard work you've spent resisting everything your body has been telling you is the most delectable item to consume! In teaching, the 'Why not?' can probably only be truly answered when you're far too immersed in it and can't actually drag yourself out. In my case it should have been answered with: it will slowly but surely drive you INSANE!

With teaching you can't enter into something so immense, eye opening and yes, possibly, life changing with such a naive view as I feel I did. Nowadays, with the many pathways available for all those who wish to jump on the train of teaching, you have an immense amount of information available to you. Schools are very open (depending on a positive CRB check/ list 99) to people sampling a little taster to see if it could be for them. There are different types of teachers who go into teaching for different reasons. Some responses to this thought-provoking question that always cause the eyes to search the right-hand side of the ceiling for an answer are:

I love kids and want to work with them

The person going into teaching for this reason will soon have their unblemished view of what children are capable of whisked away from them. The saying goes, 'never work with kids or animals'. At times in a classroom you will feel as though you are actually working with both! Yes you may meet the perfect example of a pupil: clean, polite, hard working, well equipped, bright, enthusiastic and there to learn, but they are few and far between, and even these fine well-rounded individuals can grate on your nerves with their constant need for approval to show that they are the greatest. However, the times at which you are reassured that children are not the spawn of the devil but are articulate and delightful little bundles of wonderment are really special. During the worst times, it is the memories of these little gems of energy that may keep you sane.

Obviously, you really shouldn't go into teaching with a pure and solid hatred of children as this may hinder your ability to be patient and be understanding of the many colourful and challenging ways that children can behave. You do have to want to work with children, as they are the basis of the job. You can't get away with never having to deal with the likes of a snotty-nosed 12 year old who misjudged the amount of power his sneeze would have. It's not really a 'love'. It's more an understanding, a want to aid, assist, and help to develop the skills that these mini adults need in order to function in the big bad world. With children growing up so fast and believing they are actually adults already and should, therefore, be treated as such, it's more apparent and necessary than ever before that we take a part in their understanding that, yes, maybe your mum allows you to tell her to shut up; however in the real world that will get you (a) fired or (b) slapped.

I want to make a difference

Whether you will be able to successfully achieve this, or if indeed you are able to achieve this will depend on your ego. Mr Super Ego will be of the idea that his mere presence in the classroom will cause the most delinquent of pupils to sit up and beg within a week. You also have to think of what difference you want to make and why. If you feel that you can right the wrongs done to you by your own teachers at school by becoming the best teacher in the world, remember that your view of a teacher is from the outside looking in through the sun-reflective windows. It's a very different picture on the other side. You will begin to understand more, just why your teacher went mad at you all for just talking. Why your maths teacher had you sitting next to the one person in the whole wide world that you hated with a passion. Therefore, thinking that 'I'll do it better than them' may not work out as you wanted.

If the difference you want to make is through purely altruistic reasons, then you are more likely to succeed. You just want to help. You just want the Year 7 girl (who has to get up at 5 o'clock to cook breakfast for her 27-year-old mother, and her three younger sisters because mum goes out of a night and can't cope with the morning routine) to laugh a little. Even if it's just once. That makes far more of a difference to her than ensuring she can tell the difference between a synonym and a homophone.

I enjoy the challenge

Good – because it blumming well is one! A big one at that! People may think that in order to test their limits and experience the most challenging of careers they need to join the army or something. Well look no further than your local comprehensive school. You will be tested every day. Your limits will be pushed. Every day, your capacity to stay calm when all those around you are kicking off will be severely tested. Your ability to have a smile on your face at all times despite the fact that:

(a) You've only had four hours' sleep,
(b) Your car was scratched at break,
(c) In the previous lesson you were told you resembled Shrek, will leave you feeling as though you have been an unwilling participant in a Friday night fracas.

Physically, teaching is a strain. Your energy has to remain constant, or your pupils will pick up on it and think, 'Well if she's not bothered . . .' Challenges allow us to become more skilled in problem solving and ultimately a better teacher. If you begin to stop wanting the challenge and just coast you will find yourself becoming very bored. Setting goals and meeting them also allows us as teachers, to permit ourselves the odd slap on the back. Especially, if you're hankering for a quick step up the ladder towards promotion, you must set yourself challenges that benefit the whole school as well as your individual teaching.

You will obviously be met with challenges all throughout your teaching career. It is how you respond, deal with and exceed the challenges that will make you a better or worse teacher.

Every day is different

You can never second guess what will happen on any given day. Yes you have a timetable, and yes the bell is the master of all time. However, what went before may not repeat itself, and if you are ever sucked into a false sense of security because maybe two lessons with the group from hell went well, you will dearly pay the price. That doesn't mean that you should plan for a bad lesson for every session with the class. No, in fact you should really do the opposite. You'll get used to the disappointment after a while. You really should be prepared and planned for anything. Fail to plan, plan to fail! Of course you'll be thrown the odd curve ball that no one saw coming. But generally you should have a fair idea that if it's been pelting it down at break-time, pupils will be slightly hyper (especially the girls who spent three hours straightening their hair that morning) and your starter may have to give way to some crowd control instead!

Some unplanned events that pop up can leave you laughing, crying, arguing or screaming. Whatever they are, you are sure to experience all of the above responses to a slight glitch in your day. It is certainly never boring. Some people like to have things planned and prepared for. I am one of these. Apparently, when you do one of those new-fangled cognitive tests that show you what kind of person you really are through the medium of a shape, I am a square shape! I always thought I was a circle. They don't seem as rigid and uptight, but no, there's no arguing with the shapes! I don't like changes being made to plans, but I accept that they happen. Some people prefer to fly by the seat of their pants and embrace the impromptu nature that children can bring. I am in awe of these people, I think these are the circles of life; much more relaxed.

Whether you like to feel the excitement of not knowing what lurks around the next corner, or have a mild coronary at the thought of your immaculate and best-set plans being tampered with, it will happen. Those of us who are almost obsessed with planning should prepare for the unplanned. Those who aren't, you'll be in your element.

I always wanted to be a teacher

Dressed up in your dad's suit jacket and your mum's glasses, holding a wooden spoon aloft in your left hand as you instruct Big Ted to stop pulling on GI Joe's string and that Noddy should definitely stop talking to Tiny Tears (your little sister's favourite doll). Similarly from the grand age of 4 you were teaching your Barbie dolls how to do their ten times table in your bedroom balancing in your mum's high heels whilst attempting to scratch the numbers on the board with chalk. There had never been another profession that you had even considered to waste your time on. Teaching was for you. You knew that was your chosen profession, and you'd probably never deferred from it. Oh yes, you may have had a go at sampling the delights of serving drinks, or filing papers to attain some extra income, but these were mere stopgaps. Looking upon your colleagues, some of whom had been there since the Thatcher years, you knew you wouldn't be one of them. You were going on, in your eyes, to bigger and better things.

You understood the nature of a teacher and how they should act and behave in front of the burning eyes of a group of 9 year olds; fantasizing about being the teacher who gets the apple, the enigmatic, inspiring muse at the front. As with many fantasies though, the image is always better than the reality. It is similar to fantasizing how amazingly cool it would be to be a rich and famous rock star. Money, adoration, travelling the world. What is never shown is the real picture: the 3 o'clock get-ups to get to the airport, the obsessive and somewhat scary fan who knows what colour eyes your dog has, the gruelling schedule, etc. The idea of teaching, to some, can be somewhat distorted. How hard can it be? Telling a load of kids what to do, and you get half a year off! In reality, obviously, this is so not the case. The 3 o'clock wake-ups on a Sunday morning, your mind not letting you hide the fact that you haven't planned Monday lesson one yet, the hormonal and obsessive child who has a crush on you and knows the colour of your cat's eyes. It may look all peachy from the outside – free periods! You mean you get paid to do nothing and no one's allowed to bother you? But it really isn't. If someone was to take a close-up of the face of an NQT, they would see a scowl of frustration, the grey skin of fatigue and the irritability of a chocoholic on a diet! It is a difficult profession, but if you always had your life planned as a teacher, you somehow battle through all to become that which you have always wished to be. Those bright sparks amongst you should also have done your research and realized the nature of teaching is not all 'Yes sir, no sir!'

I feel I should share my skills and knowledge for the benefit of others

If only you could get your message out to the world, the world would be a better place. It's common sense that we should all treat one another with respect. Surely it's a given that all children have the capacity to change if only they had the right person with the right knowledge and understanding of 'Yoof Culture'. All of the lessons you have learnt along the way, others should benefit from and learn to be an active and contributing member of society, just like you! At some point, you may have forgotten that since you were at school yourself, that which was once known as potential of mind that has not yet formed in a child, is now arrogance and waste. Knowledge isn't really seen as something to value, something to strive for, something to accept from those who have more of it than yourself! We now expect instant return on our investments. This includes children. Even the dreaded Inspectors of OFSTED expect an instant return on the knowledge provided by the well-versed and trained teacher and the pupil to be able to say 'I have listened to the knowledge and absorbed it and now, therefore, behold I have learnt it!' Obviously this isn't how it happens. Your extended knowledge, acquired over many years, is really of no relevance to the class staring back at you. They want to know, 'Is this the easiest way to acquire the knowledge I need to get grade C, or a level 5?' If the answer is 'no', they really won't see the need to do it. In schools now, there is a finely tuned curriculum that is designed to allow pupils to pass exams. As much as this is denied by those who still believe that they are able to stand at the front and just pour out their wisdom, unfortunately, schools are more and more becoming the 'factories' they said they would never become. Ship them in, show them how to get the magic C or L5 and ship them out again. It will be up to you to make this as exciting and enjoyable as possible; however when you wanted to pass on skills, the skills of a clown are maybe not the skills you were thinking of.

Good money

Pound signs may appear in the eyes of those who think about the security of the wage that comes with being a teacher. You think that getting paid to babysit is the best thing ever and therefore want to do it. Your ideas will be shortly dashed as you find out that teaching isn't babysitting at all and that you actually have to work very hard for the money. If you are one of those who works out how much you are paid hourly you will see that you may be contracted to 8 a.m. to 3.30 p.m., but those aren't the hours you'll work. Easy money can be better achieved by attempting to grow it yourself on a tree than by teaching, especially in your first few years. As you work your way up the MPS (Main Pay Scale) you do get more and more money for the amount of hours you have to put in. The more and more experienced you become the better pay you will get in ratio to the amount of work put in. Unfortunately, if you are the kind to start teaching for the money, you probably won't last long enough to be able to appreciate the financial benefits that will come later on in your career.

Teachers' wages have become a reason to get into the profession due to the increase and level of progression during the first ten years you are in teaching. MPS is what all teachers in mainstream education are on, those who have been in teaching and gone through threshold will be on UPS (Upper Pay Scale).

Good holidays

Thirteen weeks a year to someone outside of the educational circle will seem a ludicrous amount of paid time off. However, anyone inside that circle, anyone who does their job properly that is, will realize that without this time to gather, reflect, replenish, evaluate, drop, sod off out of the country, be away from other people's children, regain some kind of sanity, sleep, etc., we would quite possibly go under. You will recognize the symptoms of over exposure to school and pupils probably in the fifth week of a term. This ailment can be inflicted upon all who enter those school gates on a daily basis. You may suffer from lapses in consciousness, a non-existent fuse, loss of creativity, heightened cynicism, bones will feel heavy in all limbs restricting the ability to lift a pencil. Paranoia may set in and thoughts that the holidays are never going to arrive as someone is adding minutes to the hours, hours to the days, days to the week without anybody noticing it but you! Most half-terms last six or seven weeks. Every now and then you may experience the feared eight week half-term. At the beginning of this term you may think, rather naively, that you can handle it. You're refreshed from two weeks off, the sun is shining, lambs are prancing in the luscious meadows and summer is just around the corner. By week six, the holiday seems like an oasis in the arid Sahara Desert, glimmering in the haze. Your ability to construct a lucid thought let alone a lesson plan has been severely depleted and you wish each day away until the 'End of Term!'

I had a degree

You were swept up into the notion that having a degree meant you had more choice as to what job you went on to do and also that, as a graduate, you would be earning more than Dave who left school at 15 and went to work in a factory. The truth is that Dave is now the regional manager of a chain of factories, bought a house before house prices went up and earns three times what you can while you are renting digs and living the student life. You feel that you have to put your degree to some use rather than entertaining the idea that you spent three years and thousands of the pounds you didn't have to spend in the first place for nothing. Going into teaching you need a degree. Here your degree is worth something and you feel that the time and money was well spent in order for you to go into a job that actually transpires to be so far removed from what you studied on your degree that you forget how to access the memories of university after a few years anyway.

2 | Pathways into teaching

GTP, GTTP, RTP, PGCE, BED, NQT, RQT, MAD, NUTS, ETC! No my nimble fingers have not gone insane on the keyboard. Welcome to the world of acronyms! You no longer have a need for those pesky letters that make up words and that waste your precious time. In an ever-efficient world, the English language has succumbed to the 'back to basics' that has been so reverently bandied about over the last few years. It's become so basic we no longer use vowels but just the first letters of the words! To explain fully; the acronyms stand for the names of the different programmes of study available to anyone wishing to become a teacher (apart from the last two, obviously). Once upon a time you just needed to know something about something and have a reasonable wish to impart some of that something that you know to people who didn't know in order to become a teacher. Now you need GCSEs, ASs/A2s, BTECs, HONs – again, more acronyms! Of course, it is right that you should have more qualifications in order to be set loose to form the minds of children, but sometimes, having a qualification to teach isn't all that's needed in order to do the job. You can know all there is about the biomechanics of a turtle, but if you don't know how to keep a 12-year-old hormonal boy from bashing in the face of the 13-year-old hormonal boy who was seen kissing the former's 13-year-old hormonal girlfriend the night before, you may want to seek a different kind of profession. Similarly, if you don't know how to make that information on the turtle palatable for the 12-year-old hormonals, again, more education is needed. That is where the teacher's training comes in. Whatever the acronym blazoned upon it, they all really do the same thing. Prepare you for teaching. The specifics of whatever subject you are specializing in are yours to master, the nitty gritty of teaching is experienced through the many programmes.

If your aim in life is to teach, you've always wanted to teach, you believe it has always been your destiny to be a teacher – you can jump into it straight after college. The BEd courses available allow you to get a degree and a QTS at the end of it; two for one bargain you might say.

You no longer have to choose teaching the moment the umbilical cord of high school is severed at the tender age of 16. Oh no, you can decide this well into your 40s and 50s if the mood should take you! Yes the gate onto the pathways does need a lot more persuasion in order to be opened, however the number of pathways into teaching has expanded so much it's like spaghetti junction! More and more people are coming into teaching after gaining some much-needed experience in industry and at a much riper age.

Teaching programmes are delivered in many different ways. Some are college based. These are the more traditional routes of the PGCE (Post Graduate Certificate in Education) and can be studied at colleges and universities. The bait in this case is the bursary; you may be eligible to apply for £6,000–9,000, and the 'Golden Hello' you may have on offer as a nice lump sum after graduating. To those who have spent the last three years living off the pitiful wages that working behind the bar in the SU has provided, or if ma and pa have finally got sick of you sponging off them every time you need to buy 'materials', this may have you hearing the KERRCHING! Lasting one year and being predominantly theory based for the first term where you will have tutors and lots of books to read, lots of words to write, lots of advice to listen to . . . this then goes on to placements in various schools for various lengths of time. These are your ITT placements (Initial Teacher Training). You will get the chance to put that theory into practice. The first placement is only a few weeks long and normally takes place after Christmas. Being after such an enjoyable holiday and with the light of spring at the end of the tunnel should have the honeymoon period lasting at least two weeks. Honeymoon period is when the children forget it's their goal in life to make the teacher have a nervous breakdown by dinnertime instead of their parents. They do as they are told, are polite, and generally so tired after having to get up at stupid o'clock when they've been able to stay in bed until 2 p.m., they haven't got the energy to sit up let alone wind up! Here you are expected to gain knowledge and experience by watching, observing, note-taking, helping, assisting. You shouldn't be let loose on the precious children on your own just yet, but you should be watching how the pros do it!

The second placement takes place after Easter and is slightly longer, normally a term, allowing you to really get stuck into the role of teacher and get a firm grasp and ownership of a class/lesson. You are also given assignments to do that may involve having to collate data or track a child. You will have to spend at least 24 weeks based within a school for secondary teaching and 18 weeks for the primary. Throughout all of these placements, as mentioned previously, you will have mentors based at college and a member of staff at the school. Their role is to help – not babysit. Yes you will feel like you want someone to take your hand and guide you through the labyrinth of corridors allowing you safe passage to the sanctuary of the staffroom at breaktime for toast, but you really should show initiative and confidence as much as you can. Remember, you are being watched, observed, noted.

With the ever-growing use of the Internet and the ever-decreasing use of actually wanting to be in the same room/vicinity/county as someone you are communicating with let alone being taught by, you can access this programme through the OU (Open University) and also do it part time. You are still expected to do the same study programme, it is just adapted somewhat to suit.

The other popular route is to go through the GTTP/GTP (Graduate Teacher Training Programme). You get to play teacher straight away! For this route the interview process here is little stricter, but once you're through, you are straight on the job. I suppose it's like day release for teachers! You would have a day out at college where you would receive theory and training on the academic side to teaching. For the rest of the week you are . . . teacher! This may sound like madness and you may be wondering why anyone would throw themselves into it, but for some people, this is the best way. You do have to be of a certain age and have acquired the suitable qualifications prior to being accepted onto this programme, but this lends itself greatly to those who are coming into teaching a little later in life, have life skills to offer and industry experience. You don't get a bursary or a Golden Hello but you do get a wage. Yes, you will be getting a monthly salary and will be on the payroll of the school. What your salary will be is dependent on the school and what funding they get. You still get mentors and theory and lectures, but the onus is on you and getting stuck in there. Learning as you do. This is one for all you kinaesthetic learners!

Similar to the PGCE, it usually lasts one year; however there are fast track options available for those of you who are chomping at the bit! You also have the mandatory written assignments to do about how teachers teach and how pupils learn, etc., of varying length and you have to produce a mountain of evidence to prove you planned some lessons, taught the lessons, marked the work from the lessons, evaluated the lessons, learned from the lessons. It is with this that your mentors are a fantastic help.

Other programmes available
BEd (Bachelor of Education)

If your aim in life is to teach, you've always wanted to teach, you believe it has always been your destination to be a teacher, you can jump into it straight after college. The Bed courses available allow you to get a degree and a QTS at the end of it, a two-for-one bargain you might say. They do last three to four years, but it's all geared towards your ultimate goal – to TEACH!

SCITT (School-Centred Initial Teacher Training)

Similar to the GTP, but you don't get a wage. You get the bursary available to PGCE students and also a possible Golden

Hello. You spend your time in one school mostly, dabbling a bit in other placements, but generally immersed within the walls of one main school.

RTP (Registered Teacher Programme)

This is really for the more mature candidate, who hasn't got a degree, but can study to higher education level, and work in a school, and earn some money.

As you can see the government want to make it as easy as possible for anyone to get into teaching. They want you to teach and they want you to stay in teaching, so they will try and make it as easy as they can whilst still maintaining a high standard.

Which is the best programme for you?

Weigh up all of the options and suss out how your life would fit around the training system. Whether you want to be a student or you want to be a teacher, a student teacher is what will be the outcome of either. If you want to be a student, go for the college-based programmes. The environment in which you will be studying will be that of university life and tutors on tap. If you want to be a teacher, the placement-based programmes will suit you better. As mentioned before, both of these options can still be adapted to suit you. It may also depend on your financial position and whether you need a salary coming in. I wouldn't recommend having another part-time job while you are studying to be a teacher unless you are doing a part-time course. Whichever path you choose, you must be committed and have an understanding that for the first few years of teaching you will struggle to have a good work-life balance.

3 | Requirements

As a student there are many hoops you must jump through and boxes to tick. This never, ever, ends! You will question these hoops and the validity of how these help to prove you can teach; however, as with any hoop, it is there to be jumped through, and sometimes that is the only reason you may get for having to do it.

There are many requirements, but the only skill you will be developing is 'How to jump through hoops and tick boxes!' Many of these can include:

Written assignments – Just to show you can find out lots about something and write words about it.

Observations – Every few months you must actually teach an all singing all dancing lesson. These are really for the benefit of the observer more than the kids. Then you can resort to teaching the way you always did; out of a text book.

MER (Monitoring Evaluation and Review) – These are to show that you can mark four specified pupils' work in one week.

Marking – This is really to show parents that you can apply red pen every other page and scribble 'good' here and there.

Reports – You aren't actually allowed to write the truth, but in fact you can use a subtle coding system so that 'Your child is the devil reborn' actually reads as 'Josh is finding it challenging to commit to tasks in the class and creates barriers to his learning'.

Professional development – This is really a never-ending NQT year where you set targets that you would have to be dead not to be able to meet and show a bit of paper at the end of the cycle that proves it.

All of the above will be asked of you; however, the use and benefit of them to yourself or the pupils is rarely the main reason for doing it.

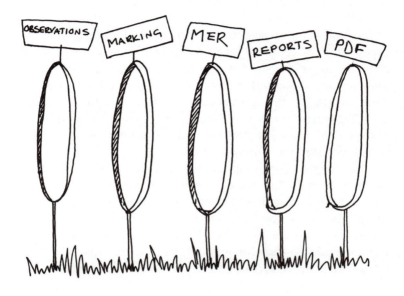

Assignments

Essays and assignments are not the be all and end all of the courses, but they are one of the hoops you have to jump through and one of the boxes you have to tick in order to pass the course. There are usually four separate assignments for whatever course you choose to take, so don't be thinking that just because you don't have to physically be in college with a lecturer bombarding you with Key Stage this and National Curriculum that, you will have less essay writing to do. Oh no, there's no getting away from it yet! It's not like a dissertation though. You won't be required to write a novel-sized report on how little Johnny in 8B has managed to regress a level and a half in the two months you had been there. The course you go on will depend on the exact nature of the essay/assignment you will be expected to complete whilst teaching and marking and planning and observing, and slowly breaking down.

Formats of these assignments can also differ. One assignment may be expected to be produced in the form of a presentation, at which point the power point comes out. It may have a word count attached to it, but this will be for the spoken word as well as the written. These are the best assignments to do as they take more research than actual writing. Some may be expected in the standard form of an essay with a word count of 2,500 words, which sounds a lot to those who are fresh out of industry and thought that their GCSE English Literature exam would be the last time they would ever have to write any more than 200 words at any one time. To those fresh out of university who will have just had to hand in a dissertation of 15,000 words, you will view this as a mere note.

Other formats for assignments can be as a project including reports and evidence of a case study you may have been working on during one of the placements; or samples of lesson plans, evaluations and pupils' marked work. Whichever course you choose to do you will have to produce some form of written evidence showing an analysis of some aspects of education. They are very difficult to fail. The tutors running the programme you have chosen to attend will have provided you with all of the information required in order for you to complete these assignments successfully. They want you to pass. The more that pass the merrier the college will be!

Lesson planning

Lesson plans can count as one part of your assignments in some courses. You will be shown many different types of lesson plans. Each teacher in each department in each school will have a different lesson plan. Once qualified, you will have some freedom in choosing the best lesson plan for you. After teaching for some time the lesson plan may be just a couple of words that have been scribbled down during the break five minutes prior to the lesson commencing, but not during training. Using the lesson plans provided by your course will feel like you may be over egging the pudding somewhat. Writing out four pages for a lesson that will last forty minutes may seem excessive, but this is a must. We all know you can plan, you know what you want to do in the lesson and when, but when all hell breaks loose because Mad Marcus in 10S has walked into your class-room ten minutes late reeking of an unsavoury tobacco sub-stance and sits at your desk, you need that minute-by-minute plan at hand to keep you on track. Whilst your mind and pulse rate are going into hyper drive as Marcus' friends decide to start a chanting session that wouldn't be out of place at a foot-ball match, your plan is still on the desk, ready to be utilized once Marcus and co have been ejected from the room by kind Mr Kneedem from the PE department. Having the incredibly detailed plan allows calm and control to commence quickly instead of thinking 'What on Earth was I doing?'

I was always told that when you start training to be a teacher the ratio of time taken to plan a lesson and the length of the lesson is directly related to the amount of time you have been teaching. Your first lesson plan can take anything up to five hours to plan, depending on resources and complication of the lesson. I have spent a whole evening cutting up a huge mix and match starter that only lasted ten minutes. To rub salt in the wound, there was no appreciation from pupils at the amount of blood, sweat and tears that had gone into typing, printing, laminating and colour coding the characters' names and quotes from *Romeo and Juliet*. Oh no, as soon as you think that they give a damn at how much effort has gone into your planning, you are on that slippery slope down to thinking that pupils within a school are human and share the same morals and ethics as you and me.

4 | Standards and evidence

The standards are the bible of the Trainee Teacher. In the standards you will find what you should be doing, how you should be doing it and when you should be doing it. They are like mini assessments that you have to complete in your training year. Due to the ridiculous number of standards one was expected to read let alone accomplish, they have gone through a recent overhaul and they have become much more streamlined and succinct. There's still a lot to meet and more's the point, a lot to prove. I started meeting certain standards even before I started the ITT course! There are certain skills and methods that are so transferable that they can easily be used to show you have met certain standards. Even the work experience you may have done five years previously in a local primary school can provide plenty of evidence for your standards.

Standards are split up into three main areas: Table 1.1

Professional values and practice	Outline the attitudes and commitment expected of anyone qualifying to be a teacher – e.g. treating pupils and students consistently; communicating sensitively and effectively with parents and carers.
Knowledge and understanding	Requires newly qualified teachers to be confident and authoritative in the subjects they teach, and to have a clear understanding of how all pupils should progress and what teachers should expect them to achieve.
Teaching	Relate to the skills involved in actually delivering lessons – e.g. planning, monitoring, assessment and class management. They are underpinned by the values and knowledge covered in the first two sections.

Professional attributes

Outline the attitudes and commitment expected of anyone qualifying to be a teacher – e.g. treating pupils and students consistently; communicating sensitively and effectively with parents and carers.

This will include anything that is part of the job as a general teacher within the school in which you are working/training. You will be expected to show that you can work as part of a team as well as have a brain that works on its own. Teams within a school can be many different things as you are the lucky member of many teams! One team will be the department you're working in. Evidence taken from this to show you have actually graced the department work room with your presence may be things like minutes from meetings where you've said something relatively important regarding information of departmental structures.

Another team of which you will be a member is that of the 'whole school'. You may hear in lectures phrases like 'whole-school issues'; this basically means 'Do you have a clue as to how the school is run?' The items, from this, to put away in the precious portfolio will be the policies the school has on uniform, bullying, meetings, the school day, discipline, rewards and anything that you may have been involved in that was outside of your department. The information in an introductory pack should really contain all of the information that no one ever reads but bulks out your teaching folder and your precious portfolio quite well.

You will also be a valid and excitable member of the ITT students. Walking around a school like a tourist in a foreign place, oohing and ahhing at the areas of the building you didn't expect to be either so vandalized or so funded by the National Lottery that it sticks out like a sore thumb! As a member of this group you have your own little tasks to complete given by the course. Although this is part of your evidence, you also have to show that you have been a valid and useful presence in the school. This can be achieved by helping with displays, assemblies or being an extra body on the rare school trips that occur nowadays, ensuring the Year 10 boys don't go trying to light up behind the posh theatre during intermission.

Dealing with parents may seem like an incredibly daunting prospect when you see the dramas on TV that show parents to be rabid animals after the teacher's blood. In actual fact, if you do it properly, it can be quite rewarding and can help build relationships that are very useful when being used as blackmail against little Max who won't even lift his eyelid let alone a pen until you mention the fact that you have his mum's mobile number on speed dial and your finger is hovering over the call button! Then he moves, oh yes!

Log any calls you make – comments made in exercise books that are sent home also count here. Try to call a parent to say their child who normally acts like a feral animal is behaving like an angel. That way the parent appreciates the communication rather than becoming bogged down with constant negatives. Talking to a parent on the phone is very different to talking to a parent at parents' evening. It takes guts to be honest about the fact that the child who, draped in ipods and mobile phones, is obviously the apple of daddy's eye and can do no wrong, is actually so very slow that they have almost regressed a year. Depending on the parent's temperament, they will either take it out on you, or take it out on the child. Never is it their fault. Never does the fact occur to them that when they allow their precious little one to stay out until 11 p.m. with her mates without completing GCSE coursework it may be their fault. No, it's either your fault because you didn't explain what they had to do, or it's the child's fault because they didn't say they even had any coursework to do.

Nevertheless, it is still important to take a stand with parents. Some bend over backwards to help you. I had the personal mobile number of one parent of a Year 11 boy so I could text her to say he'd arrived, and then to say whether he'd done any work. Others are so unhelpful you wonder if they know their child actually attends school.

All of this helps to meet the professional values and practice standard. As noted before though, make sure you keep all evidence, no matter how small. You never know how important it may be in your portfolio of evidence.

Professional knowledge and understanding

Requires newly qualified teachers to be confident and authoritative in the subjects they teach, and to have a clear understanding of how all pupils should progress and what teachers should expect them to achieve.

QTS skills test – numeracy/ICT/literacy

As we are going into the profession that is promoting and developing the need for basic skills and the 3/4 r's: Reading, Riting, Rithmatic, Romputers, it is required that we prove we are able to work out how many children would be left without a part in a play if 23 per cent of a class of 34 were working on painting the corrugated card scenery with powder paints and 4 per cent of those were doubling up as Oliver and the Artful Dodger in the Christmas production.

Whatever you are going to teach you have to demonstrate that you have the basic knowledge that everyone should have really. For some of you this will be a hurdle you can't get over easily. If you haven't studied maths for ten years and only just scraped the C at GCSE in the first place, the mathematical questions may as well be on quantum physics, or you had a personal tutor 'assisting' you with your literature coursework essays to help you get that precious C grade in English and the last time you used a computer the screen was in green and black and made a whirring static sound when loading up the Spectrum.

The good thing is though, you can re-take them until you pass, so you may be there every week for ten weeks trying to import an image from a fictitious web page onto a fictitious document even though you will be teaching food technology. You will also receive a lot of guidance and have the opportunity to complete practice tasks. The test is done on a computer where you have to listen to the questions surrounded by other would-be teachers all doing the same thing, all with a worried look on their faces, and all with their cheeks squashed in by the huge and heavy headphones you are provided with. On completion of the test there will be an assistant who will get a printout from the computer which will tell you whether you have passed or failed. Depending on the sadistic nature of this delightful person, you may be able to see whether you have passed or failed by looking at their face. Personally I failed my maths three times, each time the sympathetic face of the assistant got more and more animated. Trying to make me feel better, she started to tell me I may not be putting the decimal point in the right place, or I had put a space in between numbers. I knew it was just the fact that I was rubbish at maths when I was 11, rubbish at 14, and 16, so I knew the fact I hadn't done any maths for ten years would cause a slight hindrance. I ended up collaring a friend from the maths department at the school where I was training who had to teach me Year 9 maths in a two-hour session before I was able to walk into the test centre with my head held high in confidence, ignoring the look of pity in the eyes of the assistant. I walked out of there with my pass certificate in maths and returned to school to rapturous applause. There was more celebration over the fact that I had passed my maths than there was when I actually passed the whole training!

I strongly suggest that you practise. It is the ones who think that basic skills are skills you have naturally who will be leaving the test centre on first name terms with the assistant by the time they leave with an actual pass!

The tests themselves are quite simple. However, they are very specific to teaching tasks and aren't just general maths/literacy/ICT problems to solve. They will be about writing to parents or reading memos and creating work for lessons using ICT, but it's not in Word format so can be confusing. ICT is a massive part of teaching nowadays no matter what lesson you teach. You have to have an aspect in your lessons that lends itself to using ICT, and it is therefore necessary for you to be able to show the pupils how to do it. The likelihood of it is that the pupils will be able to write a computer programme themselves and will probably be showing you how to do the work on the computer. Don't let this damage your pride though. Inspectors and assessors love it when the pupil is able to show skills and teach other pupils, so use it to your best advantage.

Literacy is a vital part of any job, although you will wonder how on earth some people have managed to get through the interview process for some jobs when you notice on a bank statement they can't even write your name and address correctly. You obviously have to be able to read and write, although the legibility of that writing may not necessarily be of a high standard (this is where ICT comes in!). I must admit though that my spelling has never been so bad as when I started to teach English and write on the whiteboard. Questioning myself after seeing words spelt in a way even I thought impossible is all part of the job now, and the pupils are the first to spot it on the board but can't seem to manage to spot it in their own writing. Hmm. This test is really to check that you can spell and use proper grammar. If you have to write a letter to a parent, a report or even just a comment on a pupil's work that will be going home, the embarrassment of receiving marking of your own work undertaken by an overzealous parent who is probably head of English studies at Oxford, is a difficult one to live down. Difficulty lies in the way they test your spellings and grammar. The computer will show you different spellings of the same word and you have to choose the correct one. Now I don't know about you, but when I look at five different ways of spelling 'conscience' one after the other and I am panicking that I have already spent thirty seconds of the minute you're allowed to make your choice, I am going to think that they are all spelled in the right way. I will certainly have seen each way presented as the right way in pupils' books when marking them.

Numeracy is also needed in every walk of life. Again you could question this when the vacant look on the face of the shop assistant is all you are met with when you remind them that you gave them £20 to pay for a packet of chewing gum and you received £5.27 change. A grunt may also accompany the vacant look and you will wonder how they have managed to attain a position that requires basic numeracy skills. Here the tests are given to you in the form of those problems you always had in your maths exams. They always started with 'If a car drives . . .' or 'How many buckets of water . . .' With this test being for teachers, all of the questions are based on school. They all start with 'If a pupil has . . .', and 'How many pupils . . .' The basis of the whole test is about fractions and percentages but somebody felt the need to add an extra diversion. Rather than just the numerical problem you have to read through a diary about Year 10's trip to France. When you should be thinking about the percentages of how many pupils were left behind when the coach driver refused to wait longer than an hour for the stragglers, you're actually thinking about how nice it would be to visit France, or reminiscing about the trip you yourself took to France with school and thought it was hilarious to steal the PE teacher's passport and add some extra facial hair to his photograph.

You can't actually get your QTS without having passed these tests successfully so they are very important and you would be wise to get them done as soon as you can so that they are out of the way. This will leave plenty of time for you to get on with the mind-numbing task of formulating a colour-coordinated system for your portfolio of evidence so that the assessor can easily find that Post-it that has the details of a request for you to do minutes of a departmental meeting that shows how you are a valid and important member of the department!

Once you have shown you are able to spell and add up it is then necessary for you to show that you are able to get pupils to make progress. This is the biggy. Progress, progress and more progress. Even if the only thing they have made progress in is that they can now use a ruler to underline the date and title in their exercise book, it is still progress and should be highlighted and celebrated as such. It is the progress that pupils make that you are measured against. This may seem a daunting situation to be in when you have been given the bottom set art lessons to teach and find that the pupils can't even progress from eating the paint rather than using it on the paper. Don't panic though. It is not necessarily the academic progress or whether or not they have moved up from a level 4.2 to a 4.5 in an hour's lesson; it is really about whether or not they have met targets that have been individually set for the particular pupil. It's all about individual learning programmes and personal targets. If you have given Daniel Donothing a target of using at least five adjectives in his writing because he only used three in his last piece, it is whether he has met this target that will show the progress you are likely to see in your short stint as an ITT. If you think that teaching a group of 13 year olds once a week for six weeks is going to result in pupils going from a level 4 to a level 5 then you are either super human or will be doing the work for them. (This may seem like the easiest route, but is all undone when they are left on their own to do it in the exam.)

Understanding how a pupil **can** make progress and how a pupil **does** make progress are two very different things. You can't force a pupil to make progress, but you, as an educational facilitator, can aid the progress. Taking the time to get to know the pupils you are working with is vital. If you don't know what they are capable of or how they need to progress, you will not be able to provide them with the teeny tiny targets that initiate the baby steps to making progress. This section of standards is about knowledge, your knowledge.

Within this area of professional standards it also states that you need to have a deep knowledge of the subject you are teaching. This may all go out of the window once you are actually in a school after acquiring your QTS. Nowadays you are expected to turn your hand to any subject. Depending on the subject you teach and the popularity of it when Options are chosen in Year 8, you could be teaching three or four subjects. If you teach geography, but only twenty pupils choose to study it at GCSE, the school won't need five geography teachers. This doesn't mean you're redundant. Oh no. This means you are fodder for fill-in! Due to the fact that 100 per cent of the pupils in a school have to study English, maths and science it is these subjects that you will most likely find yourself teaching. You can either see this as a blessing or a curse. I found it was an opportunity to get to know other departments and also to widen my knowledge and experience of teaching. I started off teaching English, then English and art and am now running an art department. As with anything that you are thrown into in teaching, you can either see it as an opportunity to expand your professional development, or you can moan about the fact that someone thought it was appropriate to have you teaching KS3 English when your passion is French!

For your ITT placement though and in order for you to pass your PGCE you will have to have a very good level of knowledge in the subject you are teaching. For those of you in industry it is often the industry from which you are coming that will be providing you with the necessary knowledge. Any ragged edges, where your subject knowledge is concerned, can generally be neatened up with a little extra studying. This not only shows your commitment to the teaching of your subject, but will provide you with the freshest insight and all the updated information on the subject. I think all of us could do with an MOT in our own subjects every now and then to remain on top of the many changes that take place in education.

Professional skills

Relate to the skills involved in actually delivering lessons – e.g. planning, monitoring, assessment and class management. They are underpinned by the values and knowledge covered in the first two sections.

Paperwork and proof. It is here that you are proving what you say you know and understand from the previous two areas of standards. The biggest part of this, you would think, would be the actual teaching. However you would be wrong to think that. It is your planning. Fail to plan, plan to fail. As mentioned before, when you first begin writing lesson plans you will be producing a mini novel for each lesson showing that you are aware that if a fire was to break out just as you are asking Jonny to come up to the board to write down one thing he has learnt today for the plenary, you have planned the evacuation route in detail. Well, you wouldn't have to show planning for that, but you get my point. Just to add another driving analogy, as with your driving test, it is not the fact that you are not able to make a mistake; you may do a 25-point turn rather than being able to do it in three as the name suggests. No, it is if you can recover from the mistake, recognize it is a mistake and attempt to rectify it safely so as to get back on course.

Most lessons during your ITT placements are planned down to the last minute. However, if you notice that none of the pupils are actually grasping the concept that what goes up must come down then you would be making a grave mistake if you were to continue with a lesson that depends upon the pupils knowing that. The expression 'flogging a dead horse' should come to mind at this point and you should have the brains about you to think, 'I need to reassess this situation and adapt the lesson.' Planning is a necessity. However, you shouldn't be sticking to the plan at the cost of the lesson if it isn't going right for you. Even when someone is observing you and you've had to provide a plan for them, don't think that they will penalize you for straying from the plan. You will actually get more positive comments and commendations for recognizing when your efforts are lost and re-taking control of the lesson than for having a lesson that gets away from you.

Resources are a massive part of your planning. Hand-designed ones are the most effective as you can adapt them to differentiate and have them serve a specific purpose rather than just rehashing a resource that you found at the back of the KS3 filing cabinet, during the important assignment you were given to reorganize the filing system that hasn't been touched in ten years. Creating your own resources also helps to tick the box to show you are able to use ICT. You'd be amazed at the number of standards that can be cross-referenced at the mere creation of a table and an imported cartoon image from clip art to show you're a 'fun' teacher. You could even go one step further and get the pupils to create the resources and tick a whole host of boxes to do with leading learning, engaging learners and assessment for learning. Do be careful though not to overload the pupils with paper. Having a word search at the beginning of the lesson in order to engage learning straight away is one thing, but getting your daily exercise by walking around the class handing out 25 worksheets is not advisable.

The resources you draw upon should be varied and allow you to show off a variety of skills whilst enabling the most varied learning styles to be catered for. VAK is a big part of teaching today. It may sound daunting to be providing and creating resources to engage the visual, auditory and kinaesthetic learner, and it is a challenge. But when you do hit all of the learning styles in a lesson the satisfaction is worth it. When it all goes wrong and the kinaesthetic learner is taking advantage of the task that allows them to move around the classroom on a treasure hunt by climbing on top of the filing cabinet, you start to re-think the resources and activities you are capable of controlling. You can have a clear idea of how the pupils will use a resource but they will manage to find a way to use it that you wouldn't have dreamt up even at your most mischievous mindset. For example using ICT and allowing pupils on the computer is a great resource and is a necessary part of your development as an ITT student. However, if you don't explore as many of the possible ways the pupils could misuse this resource that you will be leaving them to use for at least five minutes without watching their every move, they will find a way to access all sorts of rubbish. The latest one is the tool that allows you to type in a sentence and the computer will read it out loud. It sheds a whole new light on bullying and using inappropriate language. They seem to think that because it is coming out of the computer that it isn't actually them commenting on the unfortunate weight gain and aroma that a 13 year old can experience thanks to hormones. Obviously you can't be expected to be able to stop all of these little challenges the delightful youngsters will present to you. However, if you let it be known that you are more than aware of these little tricks they think any teacher is too old and stuffy to know about, you can disarm them somewhat. As long as you put in place adequate consequences for those hardcore low-level disrupters then you are seen to be managing the behaviour in the classroom and providing a safe and effective learning environment.

You are expected to create a learning environment using all sorts of bits and pieces. You no longer teach in a classroom. You actually facilitate the learning in a learning environment. Having stimulating displays and key words strewn about the classroom adds to the environment in which learning is to take place. It may be difficult for you to be able to have much space to create your own learning environment as you will be using another teacher's classroom; however, you should still be able to use displays, like key words, that are relevant to your subject. If there isn't much on the walls then you would be meeting certain standards by creating your own display that encourages learning. Remember to take photographs of it and have it as part of your lesson plan, and to use this as evidence, as it will be quite impossible to describe its effectiveness in a few words.

Buzz words are always buzzing in and out of the education sector. The most recent one with the most impact is Assessment for Learning (AFL). This is the use of assessments to develop and encourage learning objectives and targets to be identified and met. Assessing what pupils need to do in order for them to make progress with their learning has always been a vital part in any educational setting. Now there is a title and whole policy for it. It is also another area in which you yourself are assessed as part of your own professional development. AFL should be an integral part of your lessons and should be apparent in your lesson plans and schemes of work. As this is a relatively new initiative to be standardized, being a newcomer to the world of education will count in your favour as you won't know any different. It is here that you should shine. You have the most recent training that makes sure you are equipped with the skills to be an effective teacher. In effect, you actually know an awful lot more about these new initiatives than the teachers who have been teaching for 20 years and have a coronary every time they are expected to change the way they teach in order to keep up with the times. Really, the main reason schools sign up for ITT students is to allow their own teachers to have training from you in the new initiatives that would otherwise take up a precious inset day that was earmarked to provide training in how to use the new smart boards that have finally been fitted.

Under the 'Professional Skills' heading you will be expected to show your ability to assess the progress that your fantastic teaching has 'facilitated'. This will be as well as the AFL that is expected in your day-to-day lessons. The more formal assessments you will be expected to create, mark, analyse and feedback to pupils, parents and the HoD are the ones that will produce a level. Of course you will still be expected to include this in your AFL, but this will need to be in more detail than just having a target of not scrawling over their exercise book with various images related to marijuana. With the more formal assessments you should be using NC-level descriptors to create your own assessment papers as well as assess the pupil in class. You will be expected to show you are able to use various assessment criteria and feedback using whole-school marking policies or national specifications. Peer assessments and self-assessments are one way to get brownie points, although these will differ massively from the actual level the pupils will probably receive. Just because Laura Lazylady awards herself a level 5 for her presentation about animal cruelty when all she did was bring in an RSPCA leaflet, doesn't mean that a level 5 is what will be going on the official assessment tracker sheet. What it does show is that you are empowering the pupils to analyse themselves instead of being told how they're doing by an adult. That gets you a good few ticks in a good few boxes.

Observations

Big Brother is watching you! So is your subject mentor, so is your professional mentor, so is your tutor, so is your TA, so is the teacher whose class you've taken over. Although you are being watched so often, with the constant feeling of being judged, assessed and picked to pieces, this really is a platform for you to show off. Teaching today isn't as lonely as it used to be as you will more often than not have another adult in the classroom, sorry, learning environment, with you. After a while you do become accustomed to it and can forget there is someone in there. It is at this point that you really need to be on your toes. Observers know and expect that you will put on a bit of a show for them. If you are one who thinks there is no need to up the stakes a little and show off as many skills as you can, then you won't be seeing many ticks in the ever-present boxes. Of course no one can be expected to do an all singing all dancing lesson every hour of every day. Even inspectors know this. However, it is expected, although you may be told otherwise, hence you will turn it on when it is needed. You should be given a copy of the observational record form that observers will be using to place you under a microscope and study your every word, facial expression, and movement. Use this to help you to plan a lesson in which you know you will be observed. Help the observer to tick the boxes. Look at the language used in the observation sheet and use it in your lesson. This will allow the observer to recognize the actual assessment objective you have met. Starting your lesson by announcing what the learning objective is, and asking a pupil to say why they think they are learning it, allows for at least four boxes to be ticked. I know it sounds like everything is a tick in a box, which it is, but the boxes that are being ticked are what pushes us, as teachers, to show good practice.

On an observation sheet there are approximately 50 statements/ targets that a teacher is supposed to meet in the course of a lesson. It's not impossible to meet them all; if the weather is right, if the sun is in alignment with Saturn, if the wind is in a northerly direction and if Damian Demonicson is off with flu, then the odds are more in your favour. Of course, you're not expected to tick them all and that is where your target would come in. We all have targets to meet, not just the pupils.

Observations should be planned and quite regular. If you don't feel comfortable about someone watching you teach your most dreaded class, and we all have them, then say so. Setting yourself up for failure isn't going to help anyone. If you happen to have a particularly sadistic mentor, they may want to see you with the most challenging pupils to see how you cope. In most cases though, your mentor will either help you devise lessons that will help you or observe you with a different class.

It will be through observations that you will really be able to show off all the things you understand and know about teaching. I found the most difficult part of observations was the feedback afterwards. All I wanted to say was, 'I did that in another lesson', or, 'That normally doesn't happen.' I had to accept that the observer could only comment on what they had observed. Whatever target I was given, I made sure that it was a major part of the next lesson that would be observed.

Targets have to be given. Sometimes, however, they are given just for the sake of it as it is a box that has to be filled and is a system of measuring us, as well as the pupils. Taking advice and accepting criticism is a skill in itself, especially if you don't quite agree with it. But you do have to show a level of humility and maturity, not only by taking advice, but by being seen to be actively working on those areas. This becomes difficult when you have everyone chipping in their twopence worth. Just make sure you follow the advice given by the one who has the most influence in your further career in teaching.

5 | Your Initial Teacher Training placement

Depending on the course you choose to study to take you to that precious award of QTS, you are expected to go out and about and experience as many of the different styles of schools and teaching that there are. These are your placements. The sooner you get this done, the more open your eyes will be when you chance to roam as one of us. In my opinion there is no better learning than when you try to do it for yourself. Like driving, you can say that it looks easy and that you'll easily pass the theory, but until you get behind the wheel, you don't realize how very different, and at times unrealistic the theory is. Having a computer generated image of a 4 year old running out in front of you whilst you are in the comfort of a simulator can never show you what it is really like. Not until that child does run out in front of you whilst you're changing your CD will you experience the adrenaline, shock, self-doubt and panic that come with such a horrifying situation. Theory is just that – 'in theory this should work' or 'theoretically they shouldn't react in a manner that befits a feral child'. When reading 'theory' and 'theoretically' you should remember that these are all get-out clauses for when the opposite of what should happen, does happen. We all know that it is only in practice that you can appreciate experience and learn. This is not to say that theory is useless, no, no, no! So much information is necessary to become a teacher and there is so much paperwork in particular, that theory certainly has its place. My point is really that when you walk in the shoes of a teacher for a measurable amount of time, a lot of things you thought you could either take for granted, or that you could cope with, are incredibly different in reality.

Spending time in different schools allows you to see how it is on the other side. At times you may feel that in comparison to one placement, you have genuinely moved over to the dark side, or that the grass has certainly a slightly more effervescent hint of green. Either way the point is that you get a wide variety of experiences in differing and contrasting schools.

Even before I actually chose to be a teacher I already had some experience within educational environments. This later became very useful when applying for teacher training courses as well as for jobs. I even draw on this when writing my own job applications. Primary, secondary, and post-16 are all areas in which you must have some experience, to pass your training. It doesn't matter that you don't want to do primary because the thought of sniffling ankle-biters causes your pulse to quicken and bile to rise. Nor does it matter that the mere thought of teaching secondary gets you reaching for the vodka, or the bullet-proof vest and standard issue knife-proof V-neck sweater. You have to, at least, have a go. Obviously your main placement will be at a school in which you will be amongst those that you wish to become. Even with your chosen Key Stage, you still have to experience the variations that are out there.

There can be anything up to six placements of varying lengths that you are expected to take on. These range from one afternoon a week in a primary school with a 2 per cent ethnic minority, two year groups per teacher and set in the middle of a farm, to a ten-week stint in an inner-city academy filled with hoodies and hoodlums! Wherever you are and for however long, try not to look down on any establishment or raise another on some golden pedestal. Every educational facility has its own charms and its own chains. You'd be surprised at the places where you learn the most, or that you click with instantly. More often than not, it's the schools that promote reality and have a rounded outlook on what makes a functional and independent individual, which are the places that you feel are doing the best for their pupils. Academic tables can only tell you so much about a school.

Contrast schools are your second placement, of course; otherwise it wouldn't have anything to contrast with. If your first placement is a school that achieves 92 per cent A*–C with

85 per cent Gold Standard you will be expected to spend your next placement in a school that has been stuck in special measures. So if you're sniggering at your mate who's plucked out the short straw and been given the run-down school that's an hour away from their flat for their six-week placement, while you think you're sitting pretty because you've been handed St Angels School for the divine and perfect across the road from your bedsit, think again! You will have to do your longer placement at St Lucifer's School for the feral and possessed on the other side of town!

When you first take those baby steps into the dreaded school for your ITT placement, think of it as a mere work experience. You are not there to be a teacher; you are there to learn how to be a teacher. Others around you need to be aware of this and not expect you to just set up in front of 32 children and become that that is . . . teacher. These placements are to be your first experience of what life is like in a school. Prior to this you will have read about it, written about it, talked about it, dreamt about it, had nightmares about it, had palpitations about it, had hair loss about it – you see my point. What you won't have is that rush of adrenaline that courses through your veins as you step onto the Promised Land and that first magical moment when you engage in conversation with a pupil who treats you as a teacher. Obviously pretty much any adult in an educational facility that consists of the under 16s is treated as a teacher, but don't let this stop your first feeling of 'I have finally become, that that is . . . teacher!'

It may be that your first encounter with a pupil looking up at you with such expectations causes you so much panic that you think . . . 'Can't cope!' and leave. Believe me, this has happened. It does take a person with a certain constitution to turn theory into practice.

Make yourself comfortable with your surroundings

Nowadays, and in the future it seems, schools are becoming massive, expansive educational facilities that rival the new Wembley Stadium for floor space! Being one little speck among the thousands – yes – thousands of others, is intimidating for anyone. Having the confidence that you know the shortest and most direct route to your safe haven is invaluable. All schools have different layouts and floor plans. Some are on two sites within walking distance, some are on two sites that are driving distance apart. In the latter case, unless you have your own car or moped (the second option here is only if you either want to be killed or be the butt of all the jokes) you'd better invest in a pair of roller skates or develop good relationships with those precious car owners. Thinking you can walk it, even on the most glorious of days, without damaging your back, feet and lungs is naive. The fact that the kids do it is not a gauge to measure whether or not you can.

You need to be ready, mentally and physically to stand in front of them and teach. All they need to do is sit down and get their books out. If they're red-faced, sweaty and struggling to catch their breath, it's not the end of the world. If you're clutching your chest because you've just speed-walked a mile whilst carrying a bag weighing nearly 30lb with the posture of Quasimodo, the ability to address a group of 13 year olds and get them doing brain gym is minimal. You also don't want to be relying on a 13-year-old boy whose parents you've just had in about his lack of homework to have to go on a mercy mission to find a first-aider if your body does decide to remind you of your physical limits!

The split-site issue really is a troublesome one. You don't need an extra hurdle to jump over, and when those hurdles are a mile apart, it becomes a real struggle. Complete organization is required in these circumstances and also an understanding that even the sweetest of swots will use the fact that 'they were at lower school' as a reason for being 30 minutes late to your lesson.

If you are lucky enough to have your own classroom, don't think that this means there's no need for you to have to know anywhere else. Room changes, exams, cover and the possibility of you having to teach one lesson a fortnight for resistant materials mean that you still need to know where other departments are. Meetings will also be held, at times, in the most obscure of places. Depending on availability of rooms and extra-curricular activities, you may be stuck in the stockroom discussing your ability to meet Standard 2.3.1. Embarrassment, measurable by the redness of cheeks, will occur by being that person trying to creep into the back of the room who ends up tripping over a rogue handbag causing the embarrassment to increase. Tardiness is never a quality to present yourself as having. Knowing where most rooms are will help you to ensure you're sitting there armed with pen, pencil, ruler, and diary as the chair walks in, thus gaining valuable brownie points.

Knowledge is power! If you get the chance, have a look around the school prior to your teaching. Familiarize yourself with the whereabouts of the toilets (for much-needed time to yourself), the staffroom (for regular intake of caffeine), the headteacher's office (so you can walk past and smile at them) and finally your classroom. Also get your face known around the school. The more people see you the more chance you have of being treated like a member of staff rather than patronized as a student.

If you can remember that awful feeling of panic and hysteria when your mum lost you in the supermarket that time, and then found you with snot and tears all over your face next to the Curly Wurlys in aisle 14, you'll soon know what it's like to have class waiting for you in Room Z58 while you're walking past A19 towards a labyrinth of corridors, stairs and doors and you're already ten minutes late. Arriving at Z58 with your face covered in snot and tears is not the best impression to make.

Knowing the layout of the school and where most classrooms are is invaluable. It also allows you to help the little Year 7 who also has a face covered in snot and tears and can't find where she's meant to be.

Shadow another teacher

Get a clear idea and insight into the day of a teacher. Find out what your department does at dinner; don't just stick with the other ITT students at break and dinner. This will help to show how you can become part of a team very quickly. These are also the places you will hear the real stories about the school and department! This will also help with understanding the pupils and what the general school community is like, as they all differ. You need to know if you should be bragging that you have a brand spanking new car or if you need to play it in a more humble manner due to the fact that the general community shares one Robin Reliant between them. Watching another professional allows you to steal some great little ideas and turn them into your own. You don't necessarily have to shadow a teacher in your specialism. Getting a wider knowledge of whole-school issues and curriculum really broadens your ideas. Cross-curricular ideas are becoming more and more common as is trying to act more as a team rather than keeping to separate departments. Of course, some subjects can't really cross-reference. It would just be sheer silliness to have pupils running around the all-weather pitch while reading *Lord of the Flies*, or working out whether or not Pythagoras' Theorem was of any influence on Shakespeare. Using the discipline strategies from different teachers is also interesting. Watching someone who can click their fingers and command silence; they're the tricks you want. This is yet another guaranteed form of notching up some valuable brownie points.

Copying another teacher's style or perhaps a section of a lesson is the best form of flattery. Letting them know that you were amazed at the way in which they masterfully achieved silence within seconds by holding up their hand will greatly assist in your 'likeability'. If you then say you will be using it, well, they will feel like they're 'Super Teacher', and that you're their sidekick, 'Tremendous Trainee'. It doesn't even matter if it didn't work for you. Telling Super Teacher that it didn't work adds to their ego boost that only they can have success with the 'Hovering Hand of Silence'. If it does work, they will still have their ego pumped up as they have passed on their wisdom yet again. This works best with experienced teachers who know they're good at what they do and love showing people (rubbing it in their faces). You have to pick and choose the types of teaching tactics you wish to steal and from whom. Obviously, someone who throws a board rubber at a pupil to get their attention may not be the person asked to pass on their little 'tricks'.

Listen to advice

As mentioned before, you are not expected to be 'that that is . . . teacher' in your first placement. You are there to get practice and develop practical skills. If an experienced teacher, or most likely your subject mentor, offers you advice or tries to point you in another direction – listen to them. Even if you don't agree with them, they'll have tried and tested the theory previously. So, appease them. All teachers think they have the best advice to give. A smile, a nod and a 'hmm, I'll try that' will always go down well. Obviously, everyone has their own way of doing things, however, that 'way' has been developed over many years. Having an arrogance about you that suggests you know all there is to know about teaching because you've just read the last HOW TO book on it and you got 98 per cent on your last written assignment will mean that others are quite happy to let you make mistakes. They will not help you to understand that until you are in a classroom every day and dealing with the paperwork and meetings, you don't know what teaching is. Your theory test in driving doesn't mean you'll be a good driver; it just means you can write about being a good driver. In teaching, passing your PGCE doesn't necessarily mean that you'll be a good teacher; it just means you can write about being a good teacher and you can be one for a couple of lessons a day at times. The real learning begins on the job. It takes time and learning from mistakes to discover what kind of teacher you are. Also, it may surprise you to find that you may not be the kind of teacher you thought you'd be!

Dealing with criticism

As with any training, your progress and success will be based on how well you take and use constructive criticism. Criticism is really another form of (someone thinking that they are) giving advice. As a teacher, your whole job is based on giving constructive criticism to your pupils. Due to this need for personal use, you should be aware how it can, will and may be interpreted and digested. In your role as a trainee you need to be aware of the subtle hints within criticism. Well, if the person administering the criticism has any tact at all it should be subtle anyway! You will be the one on the receiving end. Try not to read too much into the comments but do take some of the advice away with you. The better you can take it, the more understanding you will have when you come to be the one dishing it out.

There will be criticism of all areas of your work, your clothes, your hair, your accent; down to the mere essence that embodies your persona! Get used to it. This is the way you learn about yourself as a teacher. Not as a student, not as a friend, not as a mother, not even as a normal human being; but as a teacher. Once you do learn, you will find that your mind automatically critiques everyone else you come into contact with. Use this as a way to judge yourself. Once you reach this point, you should take pride in the fact that, mentally at least, you have taken a further step into becoming 'that that is . . . teacher'.

Criticism can come in many forms. It can be administered with something as simple as a mere look. Or it can be as harsh and humiliating as a staff member shouting at you in front of your class or colleagues. Take note here; however idiotic, small, insignificant, thick and useless this makes you feel, times that by ten to know how you'll make a pupil feel by blasting them in front of the class. There are two forms of criticism: constructive and just plain critical.

Constructive criticism should always highlight an area for development and in turn, help you to see how that area can be developed/constructed; the nicey nicey way of telling you where you're still an idiot and need to learn. The majority of the time this is the type used by professionals passing on their pearls of wisdom. The times at which you would expect to get these precious pearls are times such as observations, meetings and training. Here you are prepared for an ego bashing, or an ego rubbing, depending on your practice; and you're ready for it. The armour is on; your mind is asking you, 'Am I bovered?' You feel a certain protective coating shiver over your skin that allows the stinging and emotionally damaging words to slither off. You will notice, however, that whatever criticism you're given, you probably won't agree with it. Just as humans are unable to accept compliments without disagreeing with them so as to appear humble, we find it difficult to accept criticism without thinking 'What do you know?'

Critical criticism happens when a person is just telling you that you're wrong. They offer no real explanation or diplomatic reasoning. At times this is used to humiliate someone or to knock someone's confidence. This type of criticism can be incredibly damaging to morale. It is usually dished out by someone whose interpersonal skills are somewhat lacking.

Being critical of others is a natural process in all walks of life. It's how we rate ourselves. If we feel we can criticize someone else it must mean that we are more able than them. We measure our success by others' failures.

This isn't always the case though. On numerous occasions you may feel the urge to tell people to get their own houses in order before commenting on yours.

Most people are only trying to help. But because we all have our own little ways and bad habits conflicting advice may be given and you don't know whose to follow. The best way out of this is to choose the advice from the most senior person. Then at least if it does go pear-shaped, they can't really blame you.

You can ask anyone for advice. Try to establish a good rapport with the admin staff, caretakers and TAs. These will all be invaluable to you at some point. When you need advice regarding the fact that you haven't been paid it will be sorted out a lot faster than if you had previously annoyed the personnel department by getting arsy with them about the length of time it took to get the spelling of your name right. Treating your TA with respect and valuing them really earns good brownie points. This can be life saving when you desperately need some advice about how to control Bobby's tendency to launch chairs at you with unnerving accuracy.

These people know how to do things the best way. It may not be your way and it may not be the right way for you. But the advice given to you by your colleagues in priceless and shouldn't be treated with flippancy. Appreciate the advice and accept it graciously. Under your breath you can be muttering all sorts of unspeakable comments. But make them think they've saved your life with their little gem of advice and it will make them feel good. Plus it's always good to try and test advice before writing it off.

6 | Mentors

Your professional mentor

This is the person who is the official development mentor of the school. They will usually be quite high up in the food chain and they have the necessary clout that is needed from time to time. An assistant head of the school is usually responsible for development and training of colleagues in the school. They will therefore be the one mainly responsible for your training programme and induction programme in the school. Observations should be done by these mentors and meetings should be held with them on a regular basis. This person is the link between you, your subject mentor and, if on your ITT placement, your tutor at college.

During your ITT placement, your mentor will help to guide you through the basics of being a teacher and how to complete assignments and prepare your portfolio. They'll help with the cross-referencing of Standard 2.1.3 and the school trip you went on last week even though it has nothing to do with that standard. That's one of the only boxes you've not got a tick next to. They'll help you to understand how a school works, how to tackle parents' evening and how to become a well-rounded, fully functioning and operating teacher. It is their signature that is required to say you have completed your placement successfully, or not. Many don't really recover if they fall at the first practical hurdle, possibly due to the final penny dropping that, 'Maybe this isn't the best job for me!' There are two review points here, and as long as you don't get two unsatisfactory reviews you should pass. Two unsatisfactory reviews mean that you possibly, quite probably, maybe really aren't suited and should certainly hurtle down to the job centre and peruse the ads.

During your NQT year your mentor will play a similar role such as they would have done in your ITT placement. But they won't be half as nice, or patient or understanding. Don't get me wrong, they'll still be a damned sight more tolerable of you than they would a fully qualified teacher, but you have got through your training and should, therefore, have some sort of a clue. Again, it will be their signature that establishes whether or not you have passed your NQT year and can hopefully get on with moving up the ladder. During your NQT year there are termly reviews that both your subject and your professional mentor have to complete. If you get a majority of unsatisfactory reviews, you may need to repeat your NQT year. This will depend on whether or not you can, to use managerial mixed metaphors, 'dig yourself out of a sticky situation' and redeem yourself. It could also depend on the possible reasons you may have been deemed 'unsatisfactory'. If it is fixable, most schools will help you to fix it; send you on a course, observe you more, etc.

Whenever you do receive an unsatisfactory, or even a satisfactory nowadays, you will be offered advice and help to develop an action plan so you can do better next time. You may not want, ask for, or heed this advice, but you'd be daft to rebuke it. If you don't act on advice at this stage, you won't make any progress and will gradually go under with the workload and stress of failing attainment levels. If you got an unsatisfactory, you didn't do very well and therefore need to do a lot better next time or you're out matey! So, take on board whatever your mentor tells you, even if you don't agree with it. They will be expecting to see the advice, which they personally took the time out of their ridiculously busy day to tell you about, put into practice the next time they observe you with their little tick list. Well, not so little tick list, it's more like three pages of A4 both sides of tick list and comments and issues and blah blah blah!

Again they will be the ones to tell you all about how to fit in to school life and become an active member of staff.

In those cases where your tutor isn't a deputy head whose professional responsibility is for training, you may not get as full a programme of meetings, courses and general chats. But they do still have a responsibility for you. If they have been assigned to be your professional mentor, then that is what they have to take on at a competent professional level. There is the necessary paperwork they must complete and sign in order for you to progress.

Creating a relationship with your professional mentor is always advisable. This person can prevent you from becoming a teacher if they feel you don't meet the requirements. These could be concerns that only highlight themselves once you are in front of the pupils and in a school environment. You may have been getting merits in your other theory assignments, but begin to get 'not satisfactory' when you attempt to put that theory into practice. Your professional mentor is the person to decide whether or not you can make that transition from practice on paper to practice in person. It is their judgement that is the big one. If you have been struggling though, it should be your subject mentor who picks it up first, and their concerns would probably be passed on to the professional mentor, then to the course tutor. However, if you were going to be so disastrous at the front of a classroom full of children, it should really have been noticed way before you set foot in the door. There are telltale signs. A teacher can spot another teacher, or prospective teacher, a mile off. Seasoned teachers can also spot those who will never make a good teacher, even if they think they can.

Your subject mentor

This is the person attached to you who will be your first port of call during your training. The best types are usually a dynamic teacher with a few years' experience who still remembers what it was like to be in your position. They can still empathize and therefore be much more helpful. The worst type of subject mentor you can have is the dinosaur who was still around when the cane was being used. All you'll get from them is moaning about 'in my day . . .', and 'that's not constructive at all', although this may give you a quick insight into how to be a good moaner. That accomplishment will normally come on nicely of its own accord! These people are generally there just to hold your hand.

Try not to allow yourself to be drawn into some of the cynicism you may hear from a subject mentor. You'll have plenty of time to develop your own opinion of the trials and tribulations of the world of education. How your subject mentor feels about having a trainee will be seen in the quality of mentoring you receive and whether or not they attempt to burst your bubble with their pins of pessimism. Having a subject mentor who appreciates the struggle of being a 'newbie', or who believes that it is their responsibility to pass on pearls of wisdom, is obviously the better option. Unfortunately, subject mentors don't always choose the role and just see it as another thing to get in the way of their precious free time, and believe me, it is precious.

Really you should probably expect to get a mentor who does just that. In the event of getting Mrs Grumpy from Grumpyville, try to be patient and proactive. So what if you have to forge her signature on the observation form because she did it prior to the observation and had it sent to you via internal mail. It's probably a good learning curve for the future when you have to do things yourself at times when others should be doing them. As the saying goes 'If you want something doing properly, do it yourself.' Please note: obviously this doesn't apply to pupils' coursework. That would be illegal.

A good mentor may be critical, but they really are doing it to assist your own development, not just to put you in your place or see how long it is before they can make you crumble! They will take an active interest in you, nurturing you as if you were a little seedling going from the pot to the garden. You will know you have a good one when they allow you to be rubbish for the first three weeks without one negative comment. After that time, they may use phrases like 'You're really doing well, you may want to think about . . .' or 'You've made some really good progress with that class, have you managed to . . .' A rubbish mentor will blatantly tell you 'You can't do it like that, are you thick?' and other types of deflating and unhelpful comments.

Do remember though that while they are a fountain of information too much drinking from that fountain will leave it dry! In other words, you don't have to rely solely on your subject mentor; you can ask anyone in the department for help and advice.

Asking for help

If you don't ask – you don't get! Unfortunately, being teachers, if someone is quietly getting on with things we will assume that all's well. All too often, this is not the case and the person has quietly been getting on with going waaay down the wrong path! You must voice your concerns; no matter how many times you think it's a stupid question, ask it! If you don't know what to do, or need something clarifying, more trouble will be caused by not asking than by putting your tail between your legs and asking for the twentieth time how the photocopier works!

At times we all need help. You'll be surprised at what help you'll actually need when you become a teacher. Tasks you were confident in completing prior to setting foot in a school suddenly become the most arduous. You will second guess and question nearly everything you do, because that's pretty much what everyone else is doing! Do I take sugar in my tea, or do I just think I do? Did I park my car next to the bin or round by the bike stand? (If it's not in either place it's been nicked and you'll find it on the all-weather pitch the next day.) How do I write my name again? How do you spell February? What am I meant to do when I want to swear back at a child? I have never questioned myself so much, especially with spellings. Being an English teacher, asking how to spell 'assembly' can be quite a step down for me causing concern in my colleagues' confidence in my subject knowledge. One explanation for this is that throughout the day you see so many things done incorrectly by staff and pupils that you honestly question whether you do have it right, or you've just been doing it wrong all this time.

No one will actually think any less of you no matter how stupid the question. For a split second they may think, 'How do you get yourself dressed in the morning?' Especially if you do keep forgetting the things that you had a memo about, were reminded of in a meeting, were shown on the noticeboard and were re-reminded of it an hour before. We all have our limits of tolerance. However, if you really do keep asking for help without making any progress you may want to question your choice of profession.

Making an impression

You never know, you may like your placement so much that you'd like to work there. If this is the case you need to go out of your way to show the department, 'look how good I am and how much I could do for you!' Having a reputation for being a good worker will act in your favour for many years. Using the school for references and job opportunities will stand you in good stead. Make them want you! Bring in biscuits (a teacher's weak point), make the brews, help with displays, get involved. Show them they need someone like you.

In your second placement you should have more of an idea of who you are in the classroom. This does not mean, however, that this person is set in stone and that your butterfly wings can't spread a little more before you fly off to become 'that that is . . . teacher'. It just means you should have added a little more to your bag of tricks. You will still be learning the trade, so to speak. Just as with driving a car, you only truly learn how to drive when you've passed your test and you find yourself lost in the middle of a one-way system. You will truly know you are a good teacher when you're in front of 9F5, where two pupils are having a fight, and there's another climbing out of the window. Strangely no one is listening to your insightful knowledge of the uses of the apostrophe!

A good first impression is obviously the best one to make. A strong yet alluring, confident yet humble, humorous yet appropriate demeanour will always make a winning first impression. You will be scrutinized from top to bottom inside and out to see whether or not you will fit into the team. It doesn't always matter how good you are in the classroom; although commonly thought, being a teacher doesn't end when your class are dismissed. Teamwork is a must. Leaving the department still remembering you after the first meeting is a positive sign. Having them say, 'they seemed nice' may not seem like much, but believe me, teachers love moaning and criticizing the fresh meat, so anything positive from a teacher is a massive compliment.

Showing that you aren't afraid of mucking in and getting your hands dirty lets people know, you're a good un. Be armed and ready with a stapler and Blu-tack at any time. Offer to baby-sit the child thrown out for creating a weapon out of a paper towel, a pen lid and a paperclip until reinforcements arrive. Whatever help and assistance you are providing, make sure it is noticed. Without being a suck-up, all you need is that your presence has made a positive impression and has even allevi-ated some of the pressure, if only for a little while.

7 | Your Professional Development Folder (PDF)

Collect everything! Copy everything! Log everything! Once you have a room filled with schemes of work, lesson plans, minutes of meetings, observations, why you called a parent one time, quotes from many people saying how amazingly fantastic you are – then, and only then, can you know you have anything and everything the examiner will ask for.

Loads of things can be cross-referenced, and it's at this point the huge mess of papers and scribbles can be whittled down to one sheet of A4! Well not that little, but you need to have everything first to be able to sort it into what's rubbish and what's not. I used a whole room and pretty much threw anything into it that proved I existed at the school. This then became quite a therapeutic process of colour coding and labelling into four folders. Obviously, there's no need to be so anal about it, but you get my point.

Information in the folder is not only there to show that you are able to tick boxes, but how neatly and efficiently those ticks are in those boxes. A certain amount of poetic licence is allowed, as long as you can back it up or charm your way through it with the assessing tutor. Obviously they aren't going to read absolutely everything, but the easier you make it for their eye to be drawn towards the areas of your success and away from the fact that half of 7G2 actually regressed a level under your supervision the better it is for you.

Keep on top of your evidence. Try to get one piece of evidence that meets about five different standards. Label the evidence with whatever standards it meets, making it easier for allocation later. One trip to the local theatre can meet about eight different standards. One parents' evening, one phone call home, can also tick many boxes. Another good tip is to be really stingy with marks at the beginning of the year and a little more generous towards the end. In the end it all balances out, but both the child and your manager will see a progression. And that's what it's all about! The system will play you, and you have to learn how to play the system. If you accept the fact that education is really becoming a factory for producing C's in English, maths and science then you will learn that as long as these are met, you can achieve a reasonable level of reward with just the little things.

If you get the big and more difficult standards out of the way first, it may be possible to collate evidence for the smaller things in two weeks or so. If you do choose not to keep up with your Professional Development Folder you run the risk not only of failing, but not having anything to show for all of the panic attacks, sleepless nights and breakdowns of relationships at home. You would really be kicking yourself after you had the perfect lesson with Year 8 some four months ago. Alas, all you have to hand is the lesson plan you scribbled last night.

You will be surprised at the number of standards you actually meet every day without even knowing it. The challenge is to make sure you have the proof of meeting all of them. Altogether there are 33 standards to meet. Depending on your prior knowledge of these standards this number will either be quite small or ridiculously large! My portfolio consisted of seven lever-arch files that showed cross-referencing through the medium of colour! I got quite obsessed with the organization of my evidence, but that was the only way I felt confident that I had met all of the standards leaving no room for error.

During lectures and observations you will notice any literature will have on it Q4, Q8, Q9, etc. This means that it meets that particular standard and can be used as evidence to show that you have done what you should be able to do in order to be a good teacher. By the end of your first six months you will be scrutinizing everything you do and trying to fit it to a standard. Obviously there is room for some manipulation of certain evidence or situations to meet standards, but there shouldn't be a need for this. In most cases the tasks and assignments are geared towards you being able to use them as evidence in your portfolio. You only have to look at a few areas to find evidence.

Table 1.2

AREA	STANDARD	SUGGESTED EVIDENCE
ATTRIBUTES		
Relationships with children and young people (Can you be around children for any length of time without going mad?)	Q1 Q2	LESSON PLANS OBSERVATIONS
Frameworks (Do you know what goes on in a school?)	Q3(a) Q3(b)	SPECIFICATIONS SCHOOL HANDBOOK
Communicating and working with others (Can you fit in?)	Q4 Q5 Q6	PARENTS' EVENING FEEDBACK MARKING
Personal professional development (Have you made any progress whatsoever in the time you've been training?)	Q7(a) Q7(b) Q8 Q9	REPORTS FROM MEETINGS WITH MENTORS AND TUTORS

Continued

Table 1.2 Continued

AREA	STANDARD	SUGGESTED EVIDENCE
KNOWLEDGE AND UNDERSTANDING		
Teaching and learning (Can you actually do the job?)	Q10	LESSON PLANS OBSERVATIONS
Assessment and monitoring (Are you having any impact on the pupils?)	Q11 Q12 Q13	PUPILS' BOOKS FOLDERWORK ANALYSIS OF ASSESSORS
Subjects and curriculum (Do you know anything about what you're actually meant to be teaching?)	Q14 Q15	SPECIFICATIONS NC GUIDELINES LESSON PLANS SCHEMES OF WORK
Literacy, numeracy and ICT (Can you count, spell and turn a computer on?)	Q16 Q17	QTS SKILLS
Achievement and diversity (Are you aware of the challenges the pupils have before they even get through the door?)	Q18 Q19 Q20	CONTRAST PLACEMENTS ESOL CITIZENSHIP/PSHE LESSON PLANS EXTRA-CURRICULAR ACTIVITIES
Health and well-being (Can you help these pupils to stay away from drugs and underage sex?)	Q21(a) Q21(b)	PSHE LESSON PLANS FORM TUTOR NOTES
SKILLS		
Planning (Are you going into this armed and ready?)	Q22 Q23 Q24	LESSON PLANS SCHEMES OF WORK OBSERVATIONS
Teaching (Can you put your theory into action?)	Q25(a) Q25(b) Q25(c) Q25(d)	OBSERVATIONS LESSON PLANS SCHEMES OF WORK MEETINGS WITH MENTORS

Continued

Table 1.2 Continued

AREA	STANDARD	SUGGESTED EVIDENCE

Assessing, monitoring and giving feedback (Can you keep up with the marking?)	Q26(a)
	Q26(b)
	Q27
	Q28
		EXAMPLES OF WORK
		EXAMPLES OF
		  FOLDER WORK
		  MARKED
		LESSON PLANS
		OBSERVATIONS

Reviewing, teaching and learning (Can you admit when you go wrong and when you do well?)	Q29	LESSON
		  EVALUATIONS
		MEETINGS WITH
		  MENTORS
		ASSIGNMENTS

Learning environment (Can you put up a nice display and make sure the coats aren't creating a lethal obstacle course?)	Q30 Q31	OBSERVATIONS LESSON PLANS PHOTOGRAPHS
Teamworking and collaboration (Can you do as you're asked and contribute to the department?)	Q32 Q33	MEETINGS WITH MENTORS LESSON PLANS OBSERVATIONS

8 | Precious NQT status

You are now a fully fledged teacher! However you are still in 'training' and are therefore still being judged, assessed and tested and coached and monitored blah blah blah . . . However, it also means that minor mistakes are overlooked due to your lack of experience. Without using this as an excuse for everything, milk it while you can! In five years you'll think your NQT year was bliss!

The good point:
More money
The bad point:
Not enough money for what you're doing

The good point:
More ownership of classes
The bad point:
More accountability if they don't meet their target

The good point:
Chance to start developing skills
The bad point:
Making loads of mistakes and having everyone blame you for the board rubber going missing

The good point:
Beginning of a journey of self-discovery and understanding of what makes 'that that is . . . teacher'
The bad point:
Becoming aware of the red tape and bureaucracy involved in education, which means you don't actually do any educating

The good point:
Getting experience to add to your CV
The bad point:
Being given so much to do that won't count on your CV such as having to staple 300 booklets for Year 8

After passing your driving test, when your mum lets you have the 12-year-old Metro to take your mates to the cinema, you feel the same sense of freedom when you gain QTS. Just as with that old banger driven by an over-enthusiastic yet inexperienced driver, as a teacher, you learn that you need to slow down only when you have a crash. Fortunately though, you have plenty of people around you to pull you out of the wreckage of the classroom and help you get back in the driving seat. Don't be afraid to make mistakes in the classroom. This is where teaching is very different from driving! Making a mistake in the classroom isn't going to create a life or death situation. Not to sound too much like my dad, making your own mistakes is the only way you'll ever learn!

Moving up the ladder

In your first years of teaching you seem to have an urge to go out of your way to race up the ladder, at times missing valuable 'Rungs of Experience'. If you love teaching, you have plenty of time to get up the ladder. Unless you want to become an incompetent manager who has no idea how a classroom works, I suggest you get as much from the classroom as possible. It's not just the **kids** learning in there. Taking yourself out of the 'classroom' loop removes your personal input in the decision-making process. You may then be faced with ridiculous decisions being made on your behalf when you are not there to defend or challenge them. You could also end up making ridiculous decisions as you no longer have a clue about being in the classroom; it's been so long since you were in one. You would become that person who you would have moaned about just a few years before. And nobody wants to be THAT person.

The saying goes 'It's lonely at the top' and it's true. You aren't the same person as you once were. You are now . . . manager!

You annoy people with your demands and cause friction with your crazy ideas to 'reinvent the wheel'. You realize that they are only doing their job, but still recognize the 'them' and 'us' nature of management. Unfortunately, this projection of a manager is true no matter how much time has been served in the classroom.

Baby steps up the ladder are much better as you only have a minor amount of responsibility, but you feel special just because you have a fancy title that actually translates to mean 'Gopher'. It's very difficult to go back once you dive into the huge promotion pool, yet it's easy to climb out of the little promotion puddle.

Try not to spend too long in any one school unless you seriously want to see out your teaching days there. It has been known. One person I know of wished only to give six months of her precious time to a school and ended up staying there for twenty-five years. If you are applying for MPS teaching jobs after you reach threshold, unless you have a magic power that causes a blanket of silence to drape over any pupils in your presence, you become too expensive for what you can offer. An NQT will cost at least £10k less than someone who's been teaching seven years. We all know who the money-grabbing governors will choose. Plus, an NQT is much more pliable than a seasoned teacher, who's got all kinds of bad habits that they believe are mere eccentricities that allow them to bring light and divinity into the classroom. All they actually do is weird the kids out and cause them to be the new 'bullied teacher'.

If you want to move onwards and upwards, just remember, you were once in their shoes. That applies to the kids as well as the teachers!

9 | Mundane meetings

Meetings are a fact of working life. You will find that although many of the meetings are 'optional' you are required by contract to give up a certain amount of after-school time for meetings. The optional ones are ones where your absence will be noted by the chair but nothing said. Compulsory ones are those that you will get a little memo about if you miss them regularly. You will have departmental meetings, Form Tutor meetings, NQT meetings, Subject Mentor meetings, staff meetings, meetings about meetings and so on. They are a necessary evil for the mass of information your memory is required to store about various areas of the school's life.

Eye contact and nodding of the head suggests you are avidly listening to what is being said. As an NQT you may feel that your opinion may not count, but this is not the case. If you want to be a valid member of a team you need to contribute. Even if you are just reiterating what someone has said previously, at least you are showing them you have a voice. The more comfortable and confident you become the more you will feel able not only to voice your opinion but even to have a little professional disagreement. Obviously this doesn't mean you are to walk into a meeting the headmaster is chairing, shout that you think everything he says is a load of rubbish and that if he was to actually set foot in a classroom he may have a better idea!

A word of warning: during full staff meetings, other members of staff may wish to engage in creating a 'giggle' situation. Just like the kids, at the most inappropriate time someone will mention that the headmaster's toupee is wonky, or that someone had just broken wind. Just like the kids, you will have to fight with all of your strength not to get the giggles. It has been known for staff to be sent out of a meeting for such things! However, this episode did actually cause the rest of the staff to have the giggles thereafter.

We are no different from the kids really. Put a group of adults in a situation where they are lectured to and you will notice right at the beginning of the meeting that the front row is the last one to fill up, and the back row is the first row. Just as the headmaster is informing you of the GCSE results you will hear voices filtering through from the back row. There, just as with the kids, you will find the trouble-makers who are talking about the fact that the Head of Humanities who is sitting two rows in front of them is developing an ever-increasing bald patch. You will even find that notes will be passed and paper balls thrown when the SMT (Senior Management Team) are all engrossed in the statistical data that shows the school is actually performing below what they predicted and that Mr and Mrs Inspector will be giving them a roasting over that pretty soon.

Departmental meetings

These are general-focused meetings to discuss day-to-day occurrences and who's doing what. It is becoming more and more common for these meetings to entail some form of training. If you are to remember what is required of you, I recommend taking in a diary. Someone will be writing up the minutes, however for your own sanity, write down anything involving you as at times the minutes of meetings seem to be written with poetic licence!

Again, nodding of the head and eye contact with whoever is speaking shows that you're eager and actively listening (even if you're not). I find doodling in a manner that looks like I'm making notes always goes down well. This is as long as no one sees that you've actually drawn an image of department heads in compromising positions or the scrawl that reads 'This is so boring I think I'm going to have to stab my own eyes out!' Believe me, this notion will wash over you from time to time.

Just like the kids, you may be given homework and just like the kids, you are told off if you forget it and just like the kids, we have a mountain of excuses at our disposal at any time.

◆ Did you not get it? I gave it to reception to put it in your tray
◆ Oh, I've left it at Lower School (Only works on split site)
◆ Oh I've left it in my car (Only works if car park is more than five minutes away)
◆ I never got the memo (Only works if not given by hand)
◆ Was that for today? God. My Year 9s have had me so busy (Only works if you have a Year 9 class)
◆ My child was violently sick last night, unfortunately she didn't make it to the toilet and on the way managed to hit all of the marks for Year 7 (Only works if you have a child)
◆ I have them here somewhere (as you rifle through the 6-ft-high paper mountain that is your admin; they won't wait too long before saying 'never mind, give it to me later')

You could always say you have an emergency at home and ask someone to call you five minutes into the meeting, thus having to leave immediately with added sympathy from colleagues. (Only works if you are able not to feel guilty about people worrying whether your fictitious cat will survive after being knocked over by next door's toddler on a trike.)

When it comes to your turn to provide an opinion as to whether or not you should change the marking sheets from dusty blue to muted beige don't be afraid to say what you feel. If, however, you are wishing to creep, go with whatever the HoD goes with. They love it when they are agreed with, and only think you're an anarchist if you insist on arguing against them. In time you will feel comfortable and confident enough to say 'no' to the OHP marker pens and make your case for more coloured pencils.

Plan this time very carefully though. Too early and you will be known as that ITT student who thought far too much of themselves. Leave it until too late and the department will already have you branded as a 'yes' person with no backbone. You can play it safe and say nothing at all. That way you will be the ITT student that is forgotten about even before you leave the building. Also choose the issue for which your opinion will be noticed. If you are showing an overdramatic positive response to the idea of revamping the workroom noticeboard yet you actually think there are much more important things you need to be spending your time doing, don't be surprised if your enthusiasm has caused the HoD to think you'd be the best person for the job seeing as though you think it's such a good idea.

10 | Housekeeping

Organization is a major factor if you are not to go under with the amount of paperwork you will be expected to keep up to date. I am a great fan of lists. I find if I have a list, my life and work is organized. Whether or not these 'to do' lists become 'done' lists is a different matter. The cathartic nature of writing down what needs to be done really allows you to bring some perspective to your overpowering workload. If you write down what you have to do you are at least starting to acknowledge the fact that things have to be done.

The most important and useful list I've found is that of weekly 'to do's'. The feeling of pride and achievement when I can tick off a task is very positive. Even when you choose to do the mindless task of transferring marks from one page to another while marking your Year 11 coursework, it's ok. You're still being productive. You could even argue that choosing to clean out your drains rather than marking Year 11 coursework is still being productive.

The point is, if you have it on a list, you can really see what you need to do, when it needs doing and how well you're doing at tackling the tasks. A list is no good if you just keep adding to it. That's abusing the power of list making.

The power of the list goes further than just organizing your workload. In more serious circumstances it can be used to demonstrate an unfair share of workload within a department. It is also proof of your contribution to the department. Believe me, proof that you can breathe will soon be required!

Keeping copies of things also allows for reflection and ease of access if and when a parent, child or line manager requires information on a pupil. Pupils will lose things, parents will want proof that their precious little Jack is actually doing no work or homework, and keeping a copy of marks will help to prove what you say with any question asked, if you have a number ready, the person is usually satisfied.

'Jack has missed four out of six homework tasks',
Or
'I have had to give Jade five detentions in the last two weeks for bad behaviour . . . look . . . I have it written down!'

No one argues when you have it written down! Even if it's only in pencil and not blood!

Everything has its place. Try and keep all work together, homework together, pupil information together, etc. You are constantly asked to assess and provide information on your pupils to many internal and external sources. If you have these to hand, you won't look as if you have no idea who you are teaching and where they are making progress.

If you are organized you remove that flustering moment of panic when you have 32 pupils almost chanting 'MISS! MISS! MISS!' and you're flipping through a mound of paper looking for their precious work that you're sure you left on the desk before someone else taught in your classroom three days ago!

Simply put: Organization   = sanity
              Disorganization = rocking in a corner
                                muttering something
                                about 8L set 5.

11 | Special Educational Needs (SEN)/behaviour and discipline

More and more schools are being persuaded to become more 'inclusive'. Inclusion means that pupils who have Special Educational Needs of varying degrees are placed in mainstream schools. More often than not, these pupils become the bottom or 'sink' sets. Pupils with statements have more specific needs and the school receives money for them. If you have a good Inclusion Manager, they will make sure this money goes towards teaching assistants. If you don't, it goes towards getting lots of pretty coloured paper and pens for them to use and for trips out.

In theory, this is a fantastic idea. In practice it creates an unrealistic social outlook for the pupils. If a 14-year-old pupil is level 2 in a class of pupils at level 7, how can this be called inclusion when you have to create a completely different lesson for one person? Differentiation is a requirement of every teacher. This is a given. However, there comes a point when you have to think, would they feel more included with peers of a similar level and need because they realize you are 'dumbing down' the work for them?

Main difficulties faced with inclusion are behavioural. A pupil can be grade G in an A* class, but if they're well behaved and try their hardest, it makes teaching them so much easier. Difficulty arises when a pupil thinks 'I have no idea what is going on so I'm going to chew up paper, master a catapult out of a rubber band, and fire spit-sodden missiles at the geek at the front!'

These pupils are labelled as 'disaffected'. Basically, they don't care very much about their education and that's why they are nowhere near their potential grade. It's not that they've slipped through the net, but in the UK we allow pupils to go through each year and on to the next whether or not they have passed any assessments. This being the case, you get coasters who are just biding their time before they can turn 16, sign on and spend the rest of their life defying authority.

There are new labels given to pupils who are given statements every year. The first learning difficulty was dyslexia. This gave a reason as to why some pupils just couldn't make progress. All of their efforts suggested that they should but they didn't. This caused these pupils to be incorrectly labelled as unteachable and put into bottom sets. Then there was ADHD (Attention Deficit Hyperactivity Disorder) which gave teachers a reason as to why certain pupils were literally bouncing off the walls and reacting in violent and aggressive ways. At the moment ASD (Autistic Spectrum Disorder) is a major factor in SEN. ASD can cause a complete inability of these pupils to recognize social cues or to have an understanding of others around them. Their effect on others causes situations to occur in a classroom that can be quite intimidating and challenging.

Some schools have recognized that the structured school model just doesn't work for these children and have set up units within the schools that are specifically for ASD pupils. Other learning disorders that you can expect to see in a classroom will be SPLD (Specific Learning Difficulties), MLD (Moderate Learning Difficulties) and a fairly new one, ODD (Oppositional Defiance Disorder), which as far as I can tell is every child in the world! Inclusion is a massive part of mainstream schools and it is therefore necessary for teachers to differentiate. You can draw your own conclusions and formulate your own opinions as to whether you agree with inclusion or believe that pupils aren't included if they have to be taken out of a lesson to be taught. There are pros and cons for both arguments. It will depend on your ability to differentiate and have an understanding of their requirements as to whether you make that pupil feel included or not. The severity of the pupil's learning difficulty will dictate whether or not that pupil has a statement and how much money they are entitled to. Having a statement means having money for that particular child. This is for the parent as well as the school. It also means that the pupil has to have allocated time with a TA. This may only be one hour a week and will be at the discretion of the SEN Coordinator.

One way to engage these pupils is to be patient and make it sound like the task you're setting is really difficult. It's covering up that it is something that they actually may have done before but in a different way. Thinking that they're achieving is just as good as if they genuinely are. Clear instructions are also a must when dealing with SEN. Any confusion will cause frustration and ultimately the pupil will refuse to do the work. Reading it, writing it and speaking it allow understanding to be achieved.

Out of the many training sessions you will be offered, the SEN training is invaluable. The tricks experienced SEN teachers employ to ensure that someone who can barely speak their name in Year 7 can come out with a B in Year 11 are amazing. These tricks are normally incredibly simple and at times you may wonder why you didn't think of it in the first place. You may also think that you've actually tried many of the 'tricks' but Johnny is still unable to read the word 'CAT' without telling me in his own words to 'kindly leave him alone'. Patience is a huge requirement when dealing with these pupils, as is realizing that what worked last lesson may send them into a riot in the next.

Routine is also a way to encourage a comfortable atmosphere for pupils to work in. You will notice, particularly with boys, that any change will throw them. You have to explain any change, and tell them why, just to make sure they don't riot because you moved a desk. It really can be such a simple change that can cause confusion.

Behaviour and discipline

This is the main reason for the shortage of teachers and the main reason for the increase in pay. You will be bombarded with an enormous amount of rules and magic tricks to tame the beasts. Believe me, there is no magic potion! You are human and they are human. It really doesn't matter who's the adult and who's the child when you're both at breaking point. Tempers flair, regrettable statements are bandied about and tears are shed. All of these will occur in anyone's teaching career at some point.

Find your own pathway regarding discipline. What works for Mr Perfect in the next classroom may not work for you. And if anyone says, 'Ooh that always works for me', they're lying and you may feel an overwhelming urge to slap them. It's never helpful to be smug about how fab you are when someone's going under. Nothing always works straight away and every time. There are, though, a few priceless gems that we all abide by, but these are really common sense.

You are not their friend! You **are** the enemy and no amount of namby pamby teaching will change that. If you go in nicey nicey, you are setting yourself up for a public flogging. Firm but fair is always the way to go. Slackening the reins can always come later, but if the reins start off slack, it's very difficult to tighten them.

It takes time to build up any interpersonal relationship. It's the same with the pupils. They don't know how far they can push you and you don't know how far you can push them. You'll be able to push them farther, but the reaction you get from the pushing won't be as entertaining as the reaction they get from pushing you to the very edge of the chasm of insanity. Allow the time to develop relationships, so as to be able to manufacture an effective discipline structure. It pays off later as a mere look of death or raising of an eyebrow becomes as powerful as a blasting once they know what comes next.

Follow through with any sanctions that you give. If you aren't consistent with this they'll just think, 'Ah they never do owt 'bout it, so who cares cos they don't?' This also shows them you not only mean business but that you are fair. Don't have favourites. Well, we all personally have favourites and may feel like we have to take a metaphorical Valium prior to dealing with some kids, but you never let on. Kids have an amazing sense of fairness when it is directed against them. Not when **they're** being unfair though, but don't forget, their little world includes them and only them. Ours involves a whole universe.

Explain yourself and make sure they realize **why** they're being disciplined. Half the time they really are paying so little attention to the world around them they have no idea that they have just told you to 'shut up you muppet' or that they have managed to get through 50 minutes of a lesson without doing anything other than draw a marijuana leaf on the desk or perfect their make-up so they look like they've been tango'd!

Remain calm as much as you can. We all have our breaking points and there's no way you can always keep it at bay. It is a genuine physical feeling of tension and anger that builds up and warms behind your eyeballs. There is also a noticeable feeling of suppression and control when you swallow this white hot anger and frustration. You have tamed your own beast. We will all blow at sometime. It often happens when there has been a gradual build-up of events. One extra event is all it takes. You hear yourself asking why? How much more am I supposed to take? Then, from the back of the room someone throws their work transformed into an aeroplane that hits you in the head. They didn't mean to hit you in the head. In fact they are quite mortified that it has hit you and the realization of the magnitude of the situation hits them. You, however, have been pushed over the edge. But your anger doesn't come out in the form of a loud deafening tirade of chastisements. No. What actually happens has much more of a dramatic impact. You are so angry. The pupils know you are so angry and expect you to blow up. Through gritted teeth and in a calmness that chills the pupils into silence, you tell the culprit to leave the classroom . . . now. They know they've pushed you too far and recognize that it would be in their best interest to leave quickly.

It is essential to realize that, the more aggressive and angry you get, the angrier and more aggressive they will become. And so will begin the vicious cycle of teenager's vs. teacher's tantrums. Once you're in it, there's no getting out, and you aren't always the winner.

Learn their names. The power of being able to shout down a corridor and tell Neil Naughtyson to stop giving a wedgy to the Year 7 pupil with tears in his eyes is very effective. It also means that even if they run off (which they often do and remember that you should never take pursuit – teachers should never be seen running unless they're a PE teacher) you can take your time and catch them later. You let them know that you **will** hunt them down. The look on the pupil's face is very satisfying as you hand them a detention slip during their ICT lesson, apologizing to the teacher for interrupting their lesson but you had to give Neil Naughtyson this detention for bullying in full earshot of him and his peers.

No one will ever eradicate bad behaviour in schools. You did it, I did it, I'm sure the Pope and even the Queen did it. In fact, I remember having to stand under the clock for fighting when I was 8; the humiliation of having everyone walk past me knowing I was on detention was enough for me. But it's our handling of it that will help to keep us sane and safe.

School politics – how to survive in the staffroom/ the many hats

The many hats

One thing that can be said about teaching is that every day is different. Every day you will deal with all manner of different things that will test your patience, your self-control, and your stomach! In order to protect your self-worth, your feelings and your sanity there is some necessity to armour yourself. This often comes in the form of a metaphorical hat. With the hat comes a different person, a different script, and a different level of tolerance. Being a teacher you have to suppress all that makes you you. You must perch precariously on the fence. The only time I have found I am able to provide my true and honest opinion on something is with football! Working in a school in Greater Manchester and being a Man Utd supporter seems to be acceptable. You're either a Red or a Blue in my neck of the woods, and this allows for some harmless banter, but it is also a harmless opinion to hold. Obviously, as far as morals go you should always be on the side of the righteous and pure, whatever you're deepest and darkest intolerances are.

Any fears and phobias have to be swallowed and kept locked away until the crisis of the wasps' nest that has developed overnight directly outside the only window in your sweltering classroom is over! You will be amazed how you really do quash phobias when you realize that you are adding to the hysterical screaming by throwing pupils in the path of the angry, vengeful wasps. Climbing commando style over tables isn't going to help. Just deal with it by putting on your wasp-catcher hat. As a teacher, you are many things at many different times. The many hats I have worn in one day have been:

- ◆ TEACHER
- ◆ MOTHER
- ◆ BABYSITTER
- ◆ FRIEND
- ◆ MANAGER
- ◆ ME
- ◆ DISCIPLINARIAN
- ◆ AWARD GIVER
- ◆ NURSE

- PSYCHIATRIST
- COUNSELLOR
- DOG HANDLER
- BEE CATCHER
- BOUNCER
- REFEREE

Unfortunately, you cannot wear more than one hat at any one time. You may wear each and every one of them in the space of five minutes. But remember one hat has to be taken off in order for another to be put on. The most important distinction that is needed between hats is that of 'teacher' and 'me'. You cannot go into a class wearing the ME hat. You leave yourself open for personal attack and allowing your own emotions to become involved. Instead you must wear the TEACHER hat and pretty much put on an act. Your voice will be different, your tolerances will be different, and your body language will be different. It is only human though to have the ME slip through from time to time. But do beware, this can only lead to your own feelings getting hurt, or to an over-inflated ego.

You are almost like a method actor, who has to change personality to suit different situations. If you were to watch yourself teaching, and in a lot of schools, the technology is widely available to do this, you would only recognize yourself from the clothes you were wearing or the cute little scar you have just above your eyebrow caused by an argument with the wall you were always warned not to climb. It's like being possessed. At this point you probably realize you've become Mrs Bradshaw, the English teacher you used to take the mick out of for being a geek. It happens to us all. Just like we always say we're not going to turn into our mothers or fathers, it is the law of nature that we do so, much to our disgust.

When the thought of teaching is the farthest thing from your thoughts, while you yourself are looking at your English teacher and thinking 'I hate every essence that creates your being for making me write about the use of linguistic devices in *Great Expectations*' and about the choice laughed at by your careers advisor, you are actually learning how to teach. You will be surprised at the numbers of times you look to the teachers of Christmas past for advice as to how they did it. Obviously, if all you've got to go on is Mr Jones whose main teaching style was to force pupils to write in blood if they didn't have a pen and to sit at the front reading *The Times* whilst Damien Tyler strangled Ashley Manners with his shoelace, you may have to look elsewhere for inspirational teaching techniques to get you started.

The most difficult hat to wear is the MOTHER hat. Being able to console a child who has recently lost their cat or budgie is a skill only developed in someone with a vast amount of patience and care. Other instances that require you to be a parent are basic manners. You'd like to think, I'm sure, that by the time they reach you they have some form of politeness instilled, but no. Even by the age of 16, they still seem to have an aversion to saying sorry after telling you to +@?* off, or say thank you for pretty much doing the work for them. In fact, the more work you do for them, the more they will tell you, 'You never help me, you always ignore me.' Personally this is the main Teacher Tantrum button I press when I have dislocated every vertebra to help this child. There are good times when the MOTHER hat is worn. You may find a tear makes its way to the corner of your eye because Jordan has managed to recite Wordsworth even though he can't spell his name. The pride you feel can at times overwhelm you. Obviously, if your heart is made of stone, this experience may not be one for you.

Another difficult hat is that of the PSYCHIATRIST or COUNSELLOR. This comes into play when Donna and Trevor have split up and Donna is finding it difficult to accept; even after catching Trevor smooching with Janine among the *Crucible* texts in the storeroom. Or when Stacey and Kelly have fallen out because Kelly didn't invite her to the pictures on Tuesday after Stacey had invited her to Pizza Palace the previous week! Using mind games and manipulating thoughts to create a learning environment is always a valuable skill; especially when you're being observed with 8F7 after dinner and a bit of bribery is needed, or confidence boosting and positive reinforcement to get them on your side if only for an hour. At times though you really do need to try and stabilize a vulnerable 15-year-old mind such as one who has just been told on the morning of her English Literature exam that her parents are divorcing. Or a pupil hasn't done their homework because they had to feed, bathe and put to bed their three brothers and two sisters because their mum was too drunk to do it and their dad left five years ago. Understanding how to deal with a situation like this means you can provide sympathy, support and more importantly, time for that person.

With my NURSE hat on I have had to deal with the mopping up of a vast array of secretions of various bodily fluids. If you think by the age of 13 they have been potty trained, think again. They also don't seem to have managed to understand the important messages their bodies send that require urgent attention. This causes vomit to be sprayed in a trail leading to the bin/sink/carrier bag/bucket/hat, rather than in it. If you have developed a good relationship with the caretaker, they will assist in the cleaning operation quite quickly. If, however, you haven't taken time to learn their names, or smile and merrily bid good morning to them, you may be left clearing up the four hotdogs mixed with Red Bull and twenty strips of Astro Belts with the three paper towels you've found in your handbag.

By the time you are completing your RQT year your hat collection will probably rival Imelda Marcos' shoe collection. You won't have time to twirl in front of the mirror to see if the hat suits you, but try to make sure the hat fits you and that you haven't just borrowed your mate's. They never fit perfectly.

Staffroom etiquette

This is supposed to be a sanctuary where staff can casually walk in, unload their absolute hate for the Year 11 boy who has just told her to get a life when asked not to shout that Daniel's mum was begging for it the previous night across the reception, where Daniel's mum is waiting after being called in regarding his inappropriate behaviour. It is where you can swap and compare war wounds and battle scars received during the week, or where you can casually nod and smile at the people you've never even spoken to; at times maybe inform them how tired you are, or a quick 'Tsk, kids!' accompanied with eyes rolling upwards.

At breaktime it is a mass of sweaty bodies laced with the aroma of bitter coffee and burnt toast. You could call it a safe haven. It's the one place (other than the loos, and even then only at certain times) where the kids can't go. Freedom of speech is once again reinstated upon crossing from the corridor into the staffroom. You can be blunt and honest about how you feel and have a really good moan. This is what truly makes you 'that that is . . . teacher'. The ability to moan about the slightest aspect of the day, the ability to be optimistic has finally left your soul and you are at last cynical, pessimistic, paranoid and disillusioned.

As with any public space, there are rules to be followed. It may not say it on the door, or be pinned to the wall, but there normally is a seating plan in the staffroom. If this is compromised in any way, be prepared to face the wrath of the teacher who has sat in that seat for the last twenty-five years and does not appreciate some snotty-nosed little student thinking they have the right to her precious throne after gracing the school with their pathetic presence for a mere three weeks! Believe me, that seat is the only area where that person feels they have complete control. The interruption of these 15 minutes of control they have in their day can cause a nervous breakdown!

Fridge space is a commodity as valuable as residential space in Tokyo. Remember what it was like in student halls and you had to label everything so other people wouldn't nick it? This is worse! Unless you actually put a padlock on your milk, you will not see it again once you have walked away from the fridge. As teachers it is imperative that the regular shot of caffeine is administered at least 12 times a day. If that means stealing milk from the fridge, so be it. Nothing is going to get in the way of having that vital fix that will enable them to get through teaching Shakespeare's use of soliloquies to bottom set Year 11 period five.

Don't make the rookie mistake however of thinking that if they nicked yours you can nick theirs. You generally need to be as seasoned as a Kentucky Fried Drummer to have these certain privileges. It's a right earned only by time served. You will learn to appreciate it the more privileges you manage to build up over the years. There will come a time when you too will be able to get your silver service and haute cuisine menu from the canteen when you've served your time.

What is said in the staffroom stays in the staffroom. It is the ONLY place you can really say what you feel. If you overhear that Mrs Tinpot hates Kyle Klingon, it would be social and professional suicide to then tell Kyle 'I'm not the only one who thinks you're lazy, Mrs Tinpot hates you as well!' This outburst will be followed by:

(1) Parent complaint
(2) Meeting with headmaster
(3) Meeting with governors
(4) Ostracized by the teaching staff
(5) Depression
(6) Sick leave
(7) Working in McDonald's

On a more serious note, there is a slight impingement on freedom of speech. New laws have come into play that mean that if you feel the urge to set free your repressed Nazi, racist thoughts about the school's ever-growing multicultural intake, you can be reported and possibly prosecuted. Obviously, if you're stupid and ignorant enough to show this intolerant side to the greater masses, you probably deserve to be hauled up in front of the governing body and sent on a course to understand different cultures.

The same goes for sexist remarks as well. If you feel it necessary to indulge in a bit of slating of the sexes, that others find offensive, again, you can be reported and dealt with in a way that would make Bernard Manning squirm. It is really common sense that although it is a social area, it's not the local pub, and you can't get away with using the excuse that you were drunk (that would be wrong on so many levels, but still, you'd be surprised) to get away with lurid, abusive and ignorant comments.

Overall, the staffroom is a place where the real staff politics comes into play. If you're not sure which party you wish to canvass for, just look to the most powerful. As long as you are in the good books of the mighty you should be well protected. Bear in mind though that the powerful may not be the most popular! Don't completely sell your soul for the sake of first dibs on the new laptop or upgraded laptop or the new interactive whiteboards. If you are so ambitious that these things matter to you then, yes, you need a plan, and you need to be aware of who can get you an elevator up the ladder. However, try to remain true to your own standards and don't clamber and stamp over other people to get into the elevator!

Sickness and stress

As with all jobs there are stresses and strains that will test your patience and physical strength. However, it is within the teaching profession that you experience a gradual strain that is gently applied to you regularly on a daily basis, and sometimes an hourly basis. Frustrating situations are presented to you by the fact that for some reason Poppy Pedantic refuses to write in the blue pen you have provided her with as it isn't the same blue as the title is in, or that due to your extremely efficient way of working you have completed all of the marking you had early and have been asked to do the marking of Miss High-Pochondriac who has gone off sick just as Year 11 have done their mock exams. The status you want to achieve within the school will depend on how you deal with situations like this.

Being a martyr isn't an attractive feature in anyone. However, when you are trying to impress it may be difficult to say no to people asking you to, 'Can you just . . .?' or 'Would you mind . . .?' The worst one is 'You did the last one so well; can you do all of these . . .?' Saying no is a necessary requirement for your mental and physical well-being. Pick and choose the tasks you are given and don't be afraid to say if you feel you are unable to complete something. If you say yes to everything you will definitely go under. You will receive no sympathy when you go in complaining that you have far too much to do, then go on and say to your HoD, 'Of course I'll give up my weekend writing a presentation for you about how the pupils who gained level 5 did better when they ate a banana and had regular five-minute intervals of sipping freshly chilled spring water!'

If you don't listen to your body and your colleagues, you will be ill. Teaching is a very stressful occupation. A healthy work-life balance is a phrase commonly used. It is mostly paying lip service to union reps that a management team appreciates that there is a need for this. However, what I see as a healthy amount of life in relation to work, another person (head) will have been on the size 0 diet of life and the overeater's diet of work for the last ten years and will think that life should be regulated like calories: controlled and depleted.

Dealing with the lack of life you have is balanced to some degree by the holidays. What you will notice however, especially in your first year, is that just as you reach that golden half-term at the end of the mud coloured rainbow, suddenly you will feel a slight thickness in the throat. Eyes will become tired, bones will begin to ache, mucus will begin to form and amounts of it will multiply. Your body seems to know that 'I can't be ill now; I have to complete the final script for the Year 11 speaking and listening'. It recognizes that ooh, you have a holiday coming up, and you can be in bed all day! Now all of the illness that your brain and your body have been building up waiting, just waiting for the opportunity to take you down, burst into life at 6 a.m. Saturday morning. You thought you'd managed to fight off the millions of germs that Samuel Snottysneezer had fired into your face while working one to one with him. You were certain that the bug that had 'been going around' hadn't caught up with you. Well, you thought wrong.

Working in a school you are bombarded by millions of dirty, puke-producing, mucus-making, and headache-harbouring germs from every single pupil you come into contact with. There just isn't any chance of getting away from it. Oh yes, you can try Miss Lightandivinity's concoction of echinacea and St John's Wort to try and battle against germs, but you are just putting off the inevitable . . . CALLING IN SICK!

You will notice that it is the younger and newer teachers who seem to suffer most. This is because your body hasn't yet built up the antibodies to fight off the adolescents' germs. You will honestly find that very well-seasoned teachers are hardly off. This isn't because they just 'struggle through it'. No, they realized long ago that there are no rewards for coming when unwell, not being able to do the job properly and sharing their dirty germs with the rest of the department!

Every school has a different policy when it comes to calling in sick. Sick pay is very generous with schools and some people take complete advantage of this. It is also something that you will have to declare on any application form, so again be wary. If it is stress that is causing illness, get it sorted. It is a fairly common occurrence that teachers are off with stress, but it doesn't help your career if you continually are off with stress. It either shows that you are a delicate little flower and may struggle with the job, or it could show that you aren't willing to ask for help, or to try to fix the cause of the problem. You will find a school is actually very helpful when stress is taking a toll, but only if you are willing to help yourself as well.

Genuine sickness is met with various comments from all kinds of people depending on how much your absence is having an impact on the school. You have to make it as little as possible if you can. Let as many people know as possible that you won't be in. No one wants to get the news when the bell has gone and they have to find some work for your next class who were expecting a practical lesson and will now probably be spending the full hour copying out of a text book. Use any type of modern technology your weakened hands are able to get to. Text people or e-mail, let them know why you won't be in without too many fine details.

In some schools there is a system whereby you call an answering machine that is available 24 hours. These are great for those stomach bugs that cause you to spend the hours between three and five in the morning hugging the toilet. It means you can ring in after you have peeled yourself off the floor at 5.03 a.m. and crawl into bed knowing you will be able to sleep in. When you do call in, say who you are (some schools have nearly 200 members of staff), why you're not in, and when you think you will be back. In these situations it really is best to stay at home. You will do more damage by inflicting your stomach-melting bug upon your colleagues than if you stay off.

If possible though, it is a great help to suggest what work your classes can do, or even suggest they do a one-off lesson (whatever the person who's setting the cover sees fit). I was the person responsible for this at my school. A system was put into place where general cover work was in files. This cover work was so easy it didn't really require any teaching. Whatever you set though, there is no guarantee the work will be done. At times a rare creature will present itself in the form of a supply teacher who has their own guaranteed pupil pleaser that will allow them to survive the hour of battle unscathed. This normally consists of a competition of sorts resulting in the reward of sugary treats. This sends them off to my English lesson on a sugar high and a need to expel the energy by running across the tables on entering my room.

Other schools have systems where you have to call your line manager and explain how awful you're feeling. You feel a compelling urge to describe to them the exact feeling of nausea, panic and pain when you only just managed to make it to the toilet this morning, just to ensure they really believe that you are ill. People do need a certain amount of information so they can gauge how much time you will possibly need off, or whether you're a wuss who stays off because you sneezed. Obviously certain illnesses will stop you in your teaching tracks whereas someone who works behind a desk all day may struggle through. Teaching is also a very physical job, as well as taxing to your brain. Do not think you can get away with being leathered the night before and thinking you'll be fine for work in the morning. You won't, but you certainly shouldn't take time off work for it. Teaching with a hangover is like swimming in shark-infested water with a steak strapped around your back. It will only be a matter of time before your angelic Year 7s will realize that you have a hangover and turn up the volume to maximum.

Amazingly, kids know the difference between when you are genuinely ill and when you are suffering the morning after effects from that extra glass of red you knew you shouldn't have had, but it would be lonely in the bottle that had mostly been drunk. I have lost my voice many a time, occupational hazard. You'd think they wouldn't care and would pretend they didn't know you wanted them to be quiet as they couldn't hear you asking them. On the contrary, I have often had pupils quieten the rest of the class, and these generally weren't the top-setters who all want to be teacher's pet. I'd have a pupil offer to be my voice. They'd love the fact that they were allowed to shout at the rest of the class. However, I have only once taught with a hangover. As far as I was aware I hadn't even drunk that much, two, maybe three bottles of beer. Next morning I felt as though I had those teeny boppers that were only made for the smallest of skulls, clamped to my fragile head causing it to throb and pulsate violently. I was only in my first year of teaching and was still training. Thank God for the 60 per cent timetable, as I only had to teach two lessons that day and then had the afternoon as PPT. Those two hours may as well have been two days. They knew I was suffering, yet they pushed and pushed until eventually I gave in and stuck a video on. This ended up being worse; in the darkness of the room I kept feeling my eyelids close. I was suddenly startled back to reality by the screams of two pupils who had turned their pens into stabbing implements and were testing how effective they were on each other's legs.

When you say how long you may be off for, be realistic. If you have spent a full day excreting fluids from every orifice, the likelihood of you being in the next day is minimal. Don't say you'll be in the next day unless you really think you will be. It is much easier to organize a few days of work in one go than be constantly on your back foot first thing in the morning because you suddenly realized you shouldn't have tried to come into school.

In some schools they have a system that involves someone phoning you at home, or even in some cases, if you live locally, a home visit! Schools are very aware that people take advantage of the sickness pay and skive the odd day or two. But be warned, it is often easier to go into work than actually have to set work for your absence. Think of the pressure it is putting on your colleagues, whether you like them or not. If you take the mickey and are off too much, especially in your NQT year, you can fail and be forced to redo a term of your NQT year. Work will pile up and you will have more to do when you get back. Also, if you are skiving, you may need to re-think whether or not your job as a teacher at the school is one you should be doing.

You can gauge the effect of someone being off without letting anyone in the department know by listening to the general conversations when the staff realize that Mr Germmagnet isn't in on Monday morning. Complete surprise! No one had any idea until David Diligent comes into your classroom to say no teacher has shown up, or target practice, sorry, a supply teacher has turned up and there is no work left for them to have in front of them so they can chew it and decorate the ceiling in a delightful pattern of spit balls. This will result in many insulting comments about being useless and having no idea and like you don't already have enough to do without this adding to it.

Listen to what people in the department say when someone is off. If you hear things like, 'Oh I wish they'd have . . .' or 'Why do they always . . .?', remember these and try to make sure that if and when you have to call in sick that you **have** done that that they wish the others had, and that you **never** do that that the others always do that seems to irritate so much.

Whatever system a school has in place, as long as you are honest, attempt to make sure it has as little impact as possible and you keep everyone informed, then you should suffer no guilt in the genuine fact that you have not been fit for work. Saying that, I always feel guilty and often rush back to work. Don't make the mistake of going back in too early, and if you are able try to e-mail the work you would like your pupils to do. Remember, it is a job and nothing is worth making yourself ill for.

Dress code

Dress codes differ from school to school. Some are very strict and expect all staff to wear suits every day so they all look as pompous as members of the public actually think teachers are. On the other hand, some are so laid back that the pupils are better groomed than the staff. A happy medium is when you are smart yet approachable. If you look as stiff as your over-starched shirt collar the pupils won't feel they can be comfortable with you. I'm not suggesting that you turn up in your jim jams, but if you put too much armour on, the kids will put on theirs and you'll struggle to get through it.

Being too trendy can also have an adverse reaction. Depending on the type of school you're in, you may be leaving yourself open to comments from staff or pupils that it's not a fashion show and that you may suffer from a bit of vanity. Also dressing like a 50 year old if you're only 22 is seldom advisable. You won't believe the judgements that are made about you by what you wear. Nowadays, places like Primark have become the haven for teachers.

There are some obvious 'no no's' but you'd be surprised how many people think nothing of it. For the ladies, don't have a neckline lower than your collar bone. It may seem high, but remember, they are sitting down, and you are standing up. Therefore you have to bend over to talk to individuals thus giving a cracking view down your top. A 14-year-old boy and a low-cut top on a teacher do not mix. On a more serious note, you may give out inappropriate signals causing at best, a reputation with the pupils as easy, and at worst as easy and up for it.

Their hormones need no help at this age! This goes for the male teachers as well for whom a low-neck top would just be plain wrong. Skirts should always be just above or below the knee; no one wants a *Basic Instinct* wannabe in front of children.

For the men it's really the tightness and cleanliness of clothing that seems to be of an issue. Having last night's curry spread across your tie is not the way to be taken seriously. Speaking of ties, gone are the days of getting away with wearing a tie with Scooby Doo on it. Try to avoid comedy ties and other items. In a teacher, it's seen as a bit of a desperate attempt either to still be 12 years old, or to identify with the 12-year-olds. Just remember, if you have to go into a meeting with the head about a serious issue, you don't really want to be doing it with Harry Potter strapped around your neck. In primary education it's fine because that sort of thing allows very young and easily frightened children to feel a little less intimidated. By the age of 12, a pupil wants to be the intimidating one.

There are obvious occasions that are easy to dress for. It's like an unspoken law that on certain occasions you must be in a suit, wearing a tie, wearing your jeans. Times at which we have to ask, 'What do I wear?', 'What are you wearing?' you would think are only appropriate for a gaggling and giggly group of girls going out for the night and having to ring round their mates to see what they're wearing so that they don't make a terrible faux pas by wearing a miniskirt when everyone else is in trousers. But no! There are times when you will find yourself asking this question. For example:

You're going on a course. Do you wear civvies, or do you go in your work gear? You never know until you ask. Turning up in ripped jeans and a T-shirt held together with safety pins when everyone else is in three-piece suits makes you want to just curl up in the foetal position and disappear. The same goes, maybe not as dramatically mind, if you turn up in your best suit set aside for court appearances, weddings and funerals when everyone else is in jeans due to the fact they knew they would be partaking in some bizarre team-building activity that meant building bridges with a tub of wallpaper paste and last week's *Daily Mirror*.

You're going to the Year 11 leavers' do at a fancy club. Do you go all glam and look like you're trying to outdo the Year 11s who have spent the last three months not revising for their exams, but organizing their outfit and transportation to their 'Prom'? Or do you go in school gear and look like you don't know how to let your hair down? You are there as a teacher/chaperone, but you are at a special occasion. Your first experience of this will be the worst. We were a little late to the first leavers' do as members of staff due to the constant questioning of, Is this too sexy? Is this too dressy? Is this dressy enough? Generally, though, for both men and women of all ages, black trousers and a smart top/shirt will normally cover most occasions, but if and when you are unsure, ask.

13 | Going for interviews

You will have interviews at every step on your pathway to teaching. The first interview will be that of the programme you wish to study on. Whichever one you choose, you should have a script ready plus all of your relevant documentation. The script should never contain words or phrases like: 'paedo', 'power hungry', 'always hated children', or 'When do I get a pay rise?' Use your common sense and don't be afraid to ask questions. They will always ask you, 'Why do you want to be a teacher?' Do include words like: educational environment, every child matters, learning (not teaching), progress, challenging, professional, relish, etc.

The next lot of interviews should be mock interviews provided by your teaching programme. Here you are able to make all the stupid mistakes, answer questions as a person with less than one brain cell and ask those questions you never should. Remember that this normally takes place in a host school with a real headteacher on the panel. You should therefore try to be professional and polite at all times. Going back to brownie points, this could score big time! Again the, 'Why did you want to be a teacher?' will more than likely crop up. Even if the truth is that you want a job that allows you to get back home early and spend precious time on World of Warcraft, this is where a little white lie is allowed. Creative lying is a necessary evil in the world of teaching.

Obviously there are limits, and you shouldn't lie so much that you're widely known as an escaped princess from Albania who is living life as a commoner, but the odd fib or two to show you are a wonderful person who should be snapped up and employed that second is acceptable and often required.

Stealing is also a sticky area you may have to dabble into. The ideas of others (not other candidates obviously, that's just not cricket!) are a great way to put forward innovative, fresh and new ideas. When asked 'How might you plan a lesson for a bottom set class who are studying poetry?', if you have seen a lesson by someone else and have seen how successful it was, you step in that teacher's shoes and ensure you sell it: 'Well, I would ensure the pupils had a quick task to complete on their tables to allow learning to take place immediately, making it a competition, as boys may respond more positively to that . . .'

You may not ever do a lesson like that even if you do have a bottom set group of lads who have to learn 30 poems for their exams! But, you've seen it, or heard it, or know full well that that would be the best way to do it, and should therefore reel it off!

Questions they may ask

What qualities do you have that you feel would make you a good teacher?

◆ Right answer: I am confident and hardworking both as an individual as well as part of a team and feel I can aid and facilitate the development of a pupil's learning in both academic and social circumstances to assist them to become well-rounded functional members of society.
◆ Wrong answer: I have a brain and can breathe in and out.

How might you deal with a serious incident between two pupils while still ensuring the whole class isn't too disrupted?

◆ Right answer: I would ensure that all pupils were away from the physical hazard and ask a responsible pupil to get assistance from a room close by while I verbally attempt to calm the situation only getting physically involved if it was safe and necessary to do so.
◆ Wrong answer: Create a space around the main event and ask the spectators to peer assess who won the fight.

What main areas of your subject do you believe to be the most important?

◆ Right answer: The independent skills they will acquire that they will be able to transfer to other areas when there is a need for problem solving.

◆ Wrong answer: There are lots of videos we can watch about it.

What would you do if a parent complained about a homework they thought was too difficult?

◆ Right answer: I would explain to the parent that the work is set at a level that their child has the potential and ability to be able to complete. However, if their child is finding it too difficult I would be happy to sit down with their child and go through the homework with them on a one-to-one basis.

◆ Wrong answer: Tell them that a 2 year old could do it.

Why did you choose to apply to this school?

◆ Right answer: I feel this school provides the ethos and learning environment that provides a safe and welcoming atmosphere enabling pupils to develop life skills and enjoy learning.

◆ Wrong answer: It's only five minutes' drive away from my house.

How would you feel about taking on more responsibility within the department?

◆ Right answer: I would relish the opportunity to take on challenges that would enable me to further develop my professional skills and would allow me to grow as a practitioner.

◆ Wrong answer: No chance, unless you're going to pay me a load more money.

Where do you see yourself in five years?

◆ Right answer: I see myself as a successful and more experienced practitioner possibly in a position of some responsibility within the department.
◆ Wrong answer: Down the pub.

Acronyms

ADHD   Attention Deficit Hyperactivity Disorder; when the pupils get bored with the lesson before it has even started.

AFL   Assessment for Learning; yet another way to test children.

ASD   Autistic Spectrum Disorder; includes Autism and Asberger's.

EBD   Emotional and Behavioural Disorders; pupils who may be bright, but have major anger issues.

GTP   Graduate Teacher Programme (took a while to decide what you really wanted to do, should know better by now than to get yourself into this)

IT   Information Technology (the only way you get a kid to do anything now)

ITT   Initial Teacher Training (no idea what you're getting yourself into)

MER   Monitoring Evaluation and Review (where you have to prove your existence)

MLD   Moderate Learning Difficulties; pupils who struggle to be at that all-important level 5!

MPS   Main Pay Scale (the reason why you don't go back)

NC   National Curriculum (bible)

NLS   National Learning Strategy (what the government – who aren't teachers – think you should teach)

NQT   **Newly** Qualified Teacher (starting to get the picture, not yet jaded)

ODD   Oppositional Defiance Disorder; a pupil who says no a lot – so every pupil then.

PDF   Professional Development Folder (blood, sweat and tears)

QTS   Qualified Teacher Status (at last)

RQT   **Recently** Qualified Teacher (got the picture, realize it's too late to go back now because you get paid so well – see MPS)

SEN   Special Educational Needs (the kids you have to do the work in a different way for)

SoW   Scheme of Work (what you should be teaching and what you show Ofsted when they come in)

SPLD   Specific Learning Difficulties; includes pupils with dyslexia and other labels that have a specific name.

TLR   Teaching and Learning Responsibility (excuse to get paid more for doing what you've always done)

UPS   Upper Pay Spine – the wage we are all putting the years in for but will have to prove our existence to actually get onto.

VAK   Visual, Auditory, Kinaesthetic. The three learning styles that show you are planning and differentiating each lesson for every one of the 35 children you have in your class.

Plenary

Well as with any good plenary, I hope to summarize how I have hopefully met my learning objective. The aim of this book was to pass on a few hints and tips that I have accrued, developed, stolen and made up, over the years I have been guiding and helping the future educators in a very small North Western catchment area. I have tried to be as honest and straight as I possibly can be without potentially putting off those wishing to set sail in the sea of SATs or tempted to travel the tracks of tests. Being a teacher is a wonderful, inspiring, challenging profession. Its rewards are bestowed upon those who do the job properly in bucket loads financially, professionally and personally.

It may seem like the easier route to give up at times, to go back to a stress-free job sat behind a desk being told what to do so that you then don't even have to think about what you should be doing still less about what others should be doing. We have all looked at or even been the person stacking the shelves in our local supermarket and thought, 'Surely they wanted something better than that?' The fact is, maybe they did have something better, and maybe they were a teacher. Teaching may have burnt them out and stacking shelves is stress free compared to teaching, plus, the porridge oats on aisle four won't answer back!

There is real truth in the saying 'What doesn't kill us makes us stronger'. It will be difficult, it will be hard work and you will want to sack it off for going down to the pub with your mates who all seem to have easier jobs than you do. Stick with it. The only reason you should think that you can't do the job is if you are not only feeling as though you can't do it, but you are also being told by the experienced individuals around you that you can't do it. If your mentors and tutors have faith in you, then you have what it takes; believe me they will tell you if you don't. It won't be in a harsh way and you will get many chances before the final nail is in the coffin, but you really do have to be very poor not to make it through your ITT and your NQT year.

I have taught in different schools with varying age and ability ranges. I can honestly say I love teaching. This doesn't mean that I don't still find it challenging, I do. Nearly every day I am faced with a 'challenge' (read as 'argumentative and insolent youth'). I still get a buzz from standing in front of a class, excited because I think I have a fantastic lesson planned for them. Even if the lesson goes to absolute pot and is as useful as a detention for the boy whose parents always believe that he is completely innocent and angelic, I accept that it won't always go perfectly. I have noticed that wherever you go and whatever you teach and whatever ability you teach, kids are kids the world over. There is no magical formula, no magic wand. There is just hard work, determination and a belief that what you are doing is making a difference.

I hope that you have found the information in this tirade of whines and moans useful in some way and that you have been able to differentiate between the helpful hints and the tongue-in-cheek tips! I remember the little gems I used to receive from all kinds of people both in and out of the educational circle. I found it very rare that people would give out information on the short cuts and the handy hints to help you to feel you were doing the right thing. I spent so much time thinking, 'Am I doing this right?' In my opinion, far too often, advice for training teachers is all about being in the classroom. The amount of time you spend planning, in meetings, marking, making resources, etc., to the amount of time you are in front of the kids, is minimal in comparison.

I wanted to provide information based on my experiences as a trainee, a teacher, a mentor and as a head of department to encompass all that is involved in the training process. There is a lack of honest and true advice in the literal form that offers guidance on all areas of becoming a teacher, whatever you decide to do, be it rise to the top as an all-powerful head one day, or if you choose to remain on the front line and take the shots from the enemy, sorry pupils, even if you only dabble for a couple of years in order to then take full advantage of the skills you will have honed and perfected to become an OFSTED inspector and wallow in the awesome power you have over the most stubborn of teachers! Once you have acquired QTS you are pretty much sorted for life. The world will always need teachers; but it will be the quality of your teaching that will show how needed you really are.

Index